OLD MANCHESTER UNITED IN COLOUR

OLD MANCHESTER UNITED IN COLOUR

Reach Sport

OLD MANCHESTER UNITED IN COLOUR

Copyright © Manchester United Football Club

The right of Manchester United Football Club to be identified as the owner of this work has been asserted in accordance with the Copyright, Designs and Patents Act, 1988. All Rights Reserved. No part of this publication may be reproduced, stored in a retrieval system, or transmitted in any form, or by any means, electronic, mechanical, photocopying, recording or otherwise without the prior permission in writing of the copyright holders, nor be otherwise circulated in any form of binding or cover other than in which it is published and without a similar condition being imposed on the subsequent publisher.

Hardback edition first published in Great Britain in 2023
www.reachsport.com
@reach_sport
Reach Sport is a part of Reach PLC Ltd, 5 St Paul's Square, Liverpool, L3 9SJ
One Canada Square, Canary Wharf, London, E15 5AP

Hardback ISBN: 9781914197680

Photo colourisation: Andy Imrie
Editor-in-chief: Ian McLeish
Editor: Paul Davies
Words: Steve Bartram, Joe Ganley
Designer: Mark Frances
Production editor: Adam Oldfield
Cover design: Rick Cooke
Proofing: Mark Wylie

Photographic acknowledgements:
Mirrorpix, Getty Images, Alamy, Colorsport

Printed and bound by Bell & Bain.

Every effort has been made to trace the copyright.
Any oversight will be rectified in future editions.

OLD MANCHESTER UNITED IN COLOUR

CONTENTS

09-15 Introduction

16-41 Match Action

42-55 Old Trafford

56-81 The Fans

82-115 The Teams

116-173 The Players

174-199 Busby's Babes

200-237 The Managers

238-275 Glory, Glory

276-288 Index

INTRODUCTION

Celebrating a colourful history...

The task of bringing alive monochrome photos from United's past was handed to a colourisation expert, and his vivid images provide fresh views of many of the moments, characters and thrilling teams that have given the Old Trafford club a global appeal

The Manchester United story is known the world over. From the humble roots of the Lancashire and Yorkshire Railway yards back in 1878, a group of wagon and carriage workers formed a collective which would go on to become one of world sport's most famous institutions.

But, while the gist of the whole tale may be familiar, the backstory is often skated over. The Reds' pre-Second War years are invariably distilled to early successes under Ernest Mangnall and a brush with bankruptcy, while the post-war era begins with Matt Busby and the story, thereafter, is replete with detail. The Busby Babes, the Munich Air Disaster, the United Trinity, cup successes of the 1970s and 1980s before the game-changing arrival of Alex Ferguson – every step of the way was captured and preserved in black and white.

Nobody involved in the club's formation could have realistically foreseen that Newton Heath LYR Football Club (which is believed to have concentrated on cricket before switching to football!) would go on to become, renamed as Manchester United, England's most successful club. Nor was there the appetite or technology to capture high-end, colour photography of each step of the process. Thus, there is little physical commemoration of the Reds' early years. Today, of course, every second of action on the pitch is captured digitally from almost every conceivable angle, shot in high definition, while an army of photographers

OLD MANCHESTER UNITED IN COLOUR

Above: Workers from the Lancashire and Yorkshire Railway sheds in Newton Heath started the football club that would become a global sporting institution. This image is from the company's Trafford Park sheds, and was taken in 1905.

capture gloriously detailed still imagery of every moment of matchday and beyond. As the game's popularity has grown in tandem with the evolution of technology and increasing media interest, football-related content has become inescapable.

United's status as one of the biggest clubs in the world was established even before Alex Ferguson's arrival at Old Trafford, but the Reds' unrivalled success during his tenure coincided perfectly with the popularity and technological boom, ensuring that glorious colour imagery exists of 1993's inaugural Premier League title, the Doubles of 1994 and 1996, plus all points in-between. The Reds' 1999 Treble triumph was unforgettable for all those fortunate enough to witness it, but the safety net of pan-media coverage

ensured that it was there in full colour to be passed on to future generations, proof that the impossibly dramatic season did indeed unfold as told.

Manchester United is a unique football club with an identity which captures the imagination like no other. The glories speak for themselves: England's most successful club was also its first to rule Europe and the world, setting the standard to which all others could aspire. So too do the renowned managers and players: Busby and Ferguson are long-established as two of the greatest minds in the game, raising and guiding generational talents. The dark times are also all-too familiar, the horror of the Munich Air Disaster demanding annual commemoration both in Manchester and

INTRODUCTION

Munich as throngs gather to pay their respects to the 23 souls who perished, while a plaque on the footbridge outside Old Trafford marks the heroic contribution of chairman James W Gibson, who saved the club from extinction in the 1930s.

Between the headlines, however, lies a story rich in detail. And this book aims to bring some of those lesser known tales to life through newly colourised images. Led by Paul Davies and Ian McLeish from the club's media team, plus former Old Trafford museum curator Mark Wylie, a bank of black-and-white photographs was collated from photo agency archives, with a view to using them to help tell the Reds' full story.

In looking for an expert to colourise that collection, Andy Imrie – also known as *AndythePhotoDr* on social media – was approached. A proud Glaswegian with Govan roots, whose mother had attended the same schools as Sir Alex Ferguson, Imrie was perfect for the role.

"After I had to give up working in retail due to my health in my late-30s, I was at a loose end for a little while," he explains. "During that time, I came across a black and white picture of my father, who had passed away, and after being quoted a price I wasn't prepared to pay in order to have it repaired and colourised, I watched some tutorials and did it myself. It turned out quite well, I quite enjoyed it and it felt worthwhile, so I started doing more and more. I put them online and through social media this tiny acorn became a mighty oak. This 'photo doctor' persona

Above: John Henry Davies saved the club from extinction and as chairman brought in a new era, with the club renamed Manchester United in 1902 and Old Trafford opened in 1910.

OLD MANCHESTER UNITED IN COLOUR

Above: Matt Busby made his 'Babes' side continental pioneers by taking them into the European Cup in 1956/57.

Below: The Cliff Training Ground in Broughton, Salford, became the place where the skills of some of United's finest players were honed.

INTRODUCTION

"I've been very lucky in how the stars have aligned. When United came to me, they had a great collection of pictures ready to help tell a story, so it was over to me to bring those images to life – Andy Imrie, the Photo Doctor

developed and it is great to be able to bring joy to people through what I do. For them, seeing an old picture of a family member or friend come to life can bring real happiness, so it's really rewarding work.

"In the space of maybe seven years, it has led me down paths I never could have anticipated. I've been working for people all over the world, German football magazine *11Freunde*, various historical societies, working for my club, Glasgow Rangers, and of course it's been brilliant to get involved with Manchester United. I'm very grateful to Paul English, a well-known United fan and a historian of the club, who got me involved in doing United-related work. I did some work on a picture of Sir Alex Ferguson and his wife Cathy on their wedding day, which I colourised from black and white, and Paul printed it, took it to an event and gave it to Sir Alex! That was quite a thing for me. My mum always used to tell us about him, this boy from Govan doing so well, so to have that connection is lovely. That respect for Sir Alex was really where my interest in United began.

"I've been very lucky in how the stars have aligned for me. When United came to me through Paul Davies and Mark Wylie, they had a great collection of pictures ready to help tell a story, so it was over to me to bring those images to life. It was highly enjoyable to be a part of, going back through so many decades. For me, every part of the process was enjoyable because I enjoyed going back

Below: United's board of directors gather to discuss the club's fortunes in September 1972.

OLD MANCHESTER UNITED IN COLOUR

Above: Not only have many United legends been colourised for this book but legends of the game also feature, like Johan Cruyff who is shown here playing for Ajax in a friendly against the Reds in August 1983.

through the history of a proper, traditional football club. As a Rangers fan, I respect and appreciate United's story and it has been a lovely experience finding out about the club's rich history. I always knew the size of the club, but I've really enjoyed getting to see all the nuances I didn't know about."

For Reds stalwart Wylie, who retired as curator of the club's museum in 2023, the project has been highly enjoyable, meeting the initial aim of making the Reds' distant past more accessible to the modern audience, despite the obstacles involved in doing so.

"There are limitations, of course, with images from the club's early years because there simply aren't that many around," he explains, "and the quality of those that do exist wasn't always the highest standard, but this works. There are some really good photographs in this collection which look even better in colour – for instance two of my favourites are one of Tommy Manley jumping to contest a ball against West Ham in the 1930s, which is a nice action shot, and one of goalkeeper Harry Gregg stooping with the ball against Everton. It's a lovely shot, nice and vibrant, great colour contrast and it works really well.

"The aim has always been to give more

"There are some really good photos in this collection which look even better in colour… details that most people won't have seen before and it all just comes together to give a fuller picture of the club's history"

– **Mark Wylie, former Old Trafford museum curator**

INTRODUCTION

information. For example, when you see photos of the first Charity Shield in 1908 between United and Queens Park Rangers, we'll naturally think of QPR in blue and white but at the time they were actually in green and white. United famously beat Blackpool in the 1948 FA Cup final in one of the all-time great finals, but not everybody knows that United wore blue shirts that afternoon. There are other instances of wearing cherry hooped shirts or blue-and-white striped away shirts, and those are little details that many people won't have seen before and it all just comes together to give a fuller picture of the club's history."

For Imrie, the man behind the colourisation process, bringing to life Reds heroes of yesteryear has been a rewarding process, and he has clear ambitions for the effect of the book on its readers.

"I'd like people to read this book and recognise that football has always been in colour," he says. "A cup final nowadays is covered by thousands of pictures, all in colour, but that was also true back in the 1930s and 1940s, and the people who were the heroes of United back then are as relevant and alive as the current crop of heroes. There should be recognition for the old heroes of the club, so if the colour helps bring that out and flicks a switch in some minds that these people were alive and vibrant, not just consigned to flat, black-and-white pictures, and that they were as passionate about their club as we are now, then I think that's the outcome I'd be happiest with."

Where there is football, the name of Manchester United is known, and that name conjures countless familiar pictures: Old Trafford in all its glory, endless trophy lifts, innumerable iconic players celebrating unforgettable goals and moments. From Denis Law's raised finger to Eric Cantona's raised collar, from the blood-twisting brilliance of George Best to the power-packed exploits of Wayne Rooney, the pictures are there to prove their timeless excellence. Now, through *Old United in Colour*, there are new eye-catching images which shine a fresh light on the broader cast of the greatest story in English football.

Above: Retired Liverpool boss Bob Paisley travels with the United team to Anfield in December 1986, in an attempt to deter a repeat of objects being thrown at the Reds' team coach the previous season. Here he shares a joke with Alex Ferguson and Bryan Robson.

MATCH ACTION

Kits, balls, boots and stadia have all dramatically changed since the monochrome era, but one thing that hasn't altered is the passion and commitment of two teams going head-to-head… as this collection of images from past games demonstrates…

OLD MANCHESTER UNITED IN COLOUR

The more things change, the more they stay the same.

The football played by Manchester United today is far removed from that extolled by Newton Heath's founding members, but the aims of both were uniform: outfight, outplay, outscore the opposition.

Back in 1878, the Heathens were based at North Road, Newton Heath, where the playing surface alternated between stony dirt and sodden mud, depending on the day's rainfall. In the absence of dressing rooms, the players had to change in a nearby pub; a state which hardly improved upon the club's 1893 relocation to Bank Street in Clayton. There, issues persisted with the playing surface, while the ramshackle main stand was blown down in a storm in 1910. Fortunately, the club had relocated to Old Trafford days earlier, whereupon concerns over the pitch eased substantially.

Nevertheless, some of the club's finest players – the Busby Babes, the United Trinity and the Class of '92, for instance – still had to ply their trade on a turf which had more than its fair share of issues. As one unnamed first-teamer quipped when a journalist suggested that the Reds would benefit from 'home advantage' in the second leg of 1991's European Cup Winners' Cup semi-final against Legia Warsaw: "Advantage? Have you seen our pitch?"

Old Trafford's microclimate, allied to teething troubles with undersoil heating in the 1990s, provided constant posers for the club's groundsmen down the years. Under the watchful eye of current incumbent Tony Sinclair, however, the Theatre of Dreams has developed one of world football's finest playing surfaces, with United winning the Premier League's Grounds Team of the Season award four times in the last eight seasons.

The lush green baize upon which United play hasn't been the game's only substantial advancement since day one. The tools with which the players work have improved markedly. Heavy, absorbent leather footballs of yesteryear have made way for modern spheres a fraction of the weight and prone to even greater feats of aerodynamic manipulation. This makes life less predictable for goalkeepers, but at least today's custodians have been afforded the

Below: Here's an image from the 1908 Charity Shield replay at Stamford Bridge, a game United won 4-0 against Queens Park Rangers in front of over 40,000 fans.

MATCH ACTION

Above: Pancho Pearson fires in against Norwich City on 1 November 1975, the only goal of a Division One victory at Old Trafford.

"George [Best] and I would ring each other up on a Friday night and cry because we used to imagine what we would be earning if we played nowadays!"

– Denis Law

greater protection of wearing gloves since the Second World War, with the movement gaining wider popularity in the 1970s.

Apparel has evolved across the board, with thick, absorbent cotton or woollen kits making way for altogether lighter counterparts today. Never mind rain; even sweat struggles to get near players thanks to wicking technology, with breathable fabrics long-established in an era of marginal gains. Footwear has trodden the same path, with heavy leather ankle boots making way for the lightweight modern footwear which proliferates the modern game. As simple, usually monochrome kits have been replaced by complex, detailed strips, demure boots have been eschewed in favour of a rich array of vivid colours. Black boots are the outlier in today's game, often outnumbered by various neon shades as players and manufacturers look to make statements.

The exponential growth in coverage of football has steadily consumed all traditional media and dominated the advent of social media. Players have long been afforded celebrity status, but today's game is awash with greater scrutiny and rewards than ever before. As Reds legend Denis Law said: "George [Best] and I would ring each other up on a Friday night and cry because we used to imagine what we would be earning if we played nowadays!"

Unique talents such as Law and Best are among those rare players widely accepted to have been able to thrive in any era of football, including the modern game. As writer Jon Townsend posited in *These Football Times*: 'The fact of the matter is Best played without the luxuries today's footballers consider mainstays in life – proper nutrition and sport science, manicured pitches, lighter football boots, easily-deceived and forgiving referees, and a brighter spotlight – and still, he is one of the few players widely considered capable enough of being able to be devastating had he played today.'

Put the ball in the opponents' goal, stop them from putting the ball in yours. The aim

OLD MANCHESTER UNITED IN COLOUR

Above: Bristol City kick off the FA Cup final at Crystal Palace, on 24 April 1909, against Ernest Mangnall's United. Thousands of Reds fans make the trip south to watch their team win the Cup thanks to a Sandy Turnbull winner.

of football is the same as it ever was, but the means of achieving that end are infinitely broader than back then. Beyond the visible evolutions in garb and equipment, preparation is also vastly different. A pre-match glass of sherry, which usually followed on from steak three hours before kick-off, was a preparatory combination not unheard of in the 1950s, but one which is sure to meet disapproval from today's nutritionists, and that's before we get into the habit of a cigarette or two before a game or at half-time. Dovetailing with meticulously managed food intake, playing workloads are also carefully controlled to coax peak performance from modern players, a routine which falls within the squad rotation system utilised throughout the game these days and as pioneered by Sir Alex in the 1990s.

While players of the 1950s would regularly take to the pitch with a belly full of slow-digesting protein and alcohol, not to mention carrying knocks or pre-existing injuries, such conditions would be virtually impossible in today's game. Injury risks are seldom taken by managers with their players, in no small part due to larger squads and, in turn, greater adaptability according to circumstance. That wealth of options allows managers to approach their fixtures with greater flexibility than ever before.

In English football's early years, an emphasis on attack prompted a largely uniform 2-3-5 approach in formation, with full-backs occupying the roles reserved for centre-backs in today's game, then a three-man midfield perched behind an attacking

In English football's early years, an emphasis on attack prompted a largely uniform 2-3-5 approach in formation, with full-backs occupying the roles reserved for centre-backs in today's game

quintet spearheaded by a centre-forward. Tactics have evolved to the extent that it is no longer unheard of for teams to operate without an attacking focal point at all. All along the way, change has been the only constant. United's three successes in the European Cup and Champions League, for instance, have been achieved with 4-3-3 in 1968, 4-4-2 in 1999 and a hybrid of both in 2008. The 1991 European Cup Winners' Cup required a 4-4-1-1 approach to upset the mighty Barcelona in Rotterdam, and a 4-1-4-1 approach yielded success in the 2017 Europa League final at the expense of Ajax. Even in the Reds' most recent success, Erik ten Hag employed a 4-2-3-1 setup to overcome Newcastle in the 2023 Carabao Cup final. There are more ways than ever to win a football match.

While only the goalkeeper's position has been unaltered by time, the role's responsibilities have unquestionably evolved. Keeping the opposition's shots at bay is no longer the be-all and end-all of the job, with an expectation to co-ordinate attacks from their infancy, either through threaded short exchanges or measured longer passes. They are expected to cope with a variety of co-ordinated pressing from the opposition – another area of exponential growth in the game – but unlocking those presses often presents space and opportunities in which to capitalise.

The backdrop to all that happens within the game is the changing face of its rules and regulations, with introductions of the pass-back law, goal-line technology and Video Assistant Referees all marking major alterations to the sport as it has continued to grow. Allowances are made for player welfare, with five substitutions allowed in each game. Prior to 1965, United had never used a single substitute!

While squads swell, spotlights burn brighter and stakes only continue to rise, football – at its heart - remains as simple now as it was when the first-ever whistle blew.

Below: United skipper Johnny Carey leads out the blue-shirted Reds at Wembley, ahead of the 1948 FA Cup final against Blackpool - a game Matt Busby's side would win 4-2.

OLD MANCHESTER UNITED IN COLOUR

Left: On 16 January 1926, the referee does the coin toss on a snow-covered Highbury pitch ahead of a First Division match between Arsenal and United. The Gunners won the game 3-2.

Right: Arsenal (in red) threaten the United goal in a top-flight fixture at Manor Field on 5 April 1912. United are wearing blue and white stripes as their change strip, with goalkeeper Hugh Edmonds donning a flat cap for this Good Friday fixture.

MATCH ACTION

United's superstar winger Billy Meredith keeps the ball in play during the 1908 Charity Shield match, the first ever played, against Queens Park Rangers. This game (in April 1908) ended as a 1-1 draw, with Meredith the Reds' scorer, but United won the replay 4-0 four months later. Both games were played at Chelsea's Stamford Bridge.

OLD MANCHESTER UNITED IN COLOUR

United and Fulham battle it out in the second of three FA Cup intermediate round ties played between the clubs in January 1905. The first of the trilogy ended as a 2-2 draw at Bank Street, followed by this first replay in front of 15,000 fans which ended goalless at Craven Cottage. In the photo, United goalkeeper Harry Moger watches the ball as it loops high in the air as the hosts seek a breakthrough. After this stalemate, a second replay took place on the neutral turf of Villa Park and this time there was finally a winner. Sadly, that was not United; Bobby Graham giving the Londoners a 1-0 win in front of 6,000 fans.

OLD MANCHESTER UNITED IN COLOUR

Derby day with a difference. United and City meet in Sheffield on 27 March 1926 in an FA Cup semi-final. League form suggests that a Reds victory was on the cards, with John Chapman's United comfortably in the top half of the First Division while City were fighting relegation. However, Cup football is anything but predictable and the Blues pull off a resounding 3-0 win in front of a 36,450 crowd. City were to suffer final defeat to Bolton Wanderers at Wembley, which was then compounded by relegation to the Second Division.

OLD MANCHESTER UNITED IN COLOUR

MATCH ACTION

No, this isn't a mistake; Manchester United really do feature in this photograph. The cherry red and white hoops might not be a kit we're familiar with but it was actually the change strip from 1932-36. Here, United are wearing the away shirt at the Boleyn Ground against West Ham on 7 March 1936. United's Tommy Manley and the Hammers' Jimmy Ruffell compete for the ball in the air in this Second Division promotion battle, which was won 2-1 by Scott Duncan's Reds thanks to goals from George Mutch and William Bryant. The victory proved a key moment in United's promotion drive, with Scott's side pipping Charlton Athletic to the Second Division title by a single point (with West Ham eventually finishing fourth).

OLD MANCHESTER UNITED IN COLOUR

Derby day at Maine Road on 20 September 1947. Manchester City captain Bert Sproston (left) shakes hands with United's Johnny Carey ahead of a goalless league draw watched by 71,364. Both sides played at the Blues' stadium from 1945-49, with Old Trafford unusable due to bomb damage. This game was City's designated home match, with the reverse fixture also ending as a draw (1-1).

MATCH ACTION

Left: United winger Charlie Mitten fires a shot at Manchester City's Bert Trautmann in a Maine Road derby on New Year's Eve 1949, having beaten Blues defender Billy Walsh to the ball. United win 2-1.

Right: Goalkeeper Ray Wood receives treatment after being shoulder charged by Aston Villa's Peter McParland just six minutes into the 1957 FA Cup final at Wembley. Wood suffers a broken cheekbone and United are forced to play much of the game with 10 men. Villa go on to win the game 2-1 with a McParland brace.

OLD MANCHESTER UNITED IN COLOUR

United goalkeeper Harry Gregg prepares to take a goal kick in this First Division home match against Everton on 7 March 1959. It had been 13 months since the Northern Irishman had survived the Munich Air Disaster, and he was now playing a key part in the rebuild being undertaken by Matt Busby and Jimmy Murphy. This particular game was won 2-1, with a 51,254 crowd seeing Freddie Goodwin and Albert Scanlon scoring for the Reds and Ronnie Cope netting an own goal for the visitors' consolation strike. Amazingly, United would eventually finish in second place in the First Division behind champions Wolverhampton Wanderers – a remarkable achievement given the huge change of personnel required after the accident.

MATCH ACTION

OLD MANCHESTER UNITED IN COLOUR

Right: United's players are mobbed after the final whistle of the 1963 FA Cup semi-final against Southampton at Villa Park on 27 April 1963. A Denis Law strike proves enough to take the Reds to Wembley in a 1-0 win.

Left: Reds stopper David? Gaskell catches a cross at Craven Cottage in September 1964, although Fulham would go on to win this First Division game 2-1. Thankfully better times awaited Matt Busby's improving side, with United eventually finishing as league champions ahead of Leeds.

MATCH ACTION

Alex Stepney warms up before a home game in the 1967/68 season, watched on by team-mate George Best. The Londoner joined the Reds in 1966 and would go on to play 539 games for United, winning one league title, the FA Cup and European Cup.

OLD MANCHESTER UNITED IN COLOUR

What a sight for the Old Trafford crowd... although a somewhat less welcome one for the opposition! Denis Law and George Best take to the hallowed turf for a home fixture in 1965/66, the pair being two thirds of what would become known at the United Trinity (completed by Bobby Charlton, of course). Reds fans were not short of potential idols in this period, with Law and Charlton already established stars, Best fast emerging as one of the game's great talents, with Matt Busby's side also including dependable and popular contributors like Nobby Stiles, Paddy Crerand and Tony Dunne. When comparing United sides from different eras, you'd be hard pressed to find a more flair-filled side than the one that won league titles in 1965 and 1967, then became English football's first European Cup winners.

MATCH ACTION

OLD MANCHESTER UNITED IN COLOUR

Left: Denis Law battles it out with Chelsea's Terry Venables and Ron Harris at Stamford Bridge on 12 March 1966.

Right: Here's Law again, but this time in the blue of Manchester City, having switched Manchester clubs in summer 1973. He's embraced by United fans despite having scored a backheel against the already relegated Reds on 27 April 1974.

MATCH ACTION

Left: Gordon Hill celebrates giving United the lead against Arsenal at Old Trafford in a Division One fixture in 1977/78. The London-born winger, signed from Millwall in 1975, was affectionately known as 'King of all Cockneys' by members of the Red Army.

Right: Players and fans celebrate at the Dell on 26 February 1977, as United force a replay against FA Cup holders Southampton. Lou Macari holds his arm aloft, and is hugged by Sammy McIlroy, after putting the Reds ahead in the fifth-round tie. United win the replay 2-1 and go on to lift the Cup.

OLD MANCHESTER UNITED IN COLOUR

MATCH ACTION

Although colour photography was increasingly taking over by the late 1980s, this image from 17 April 1985 is one that is only usually seen in monochrome. The photo shows Mark Hughes celebrating his winning goal against Liverpool in an FA Cup semi-final replay, the first game having ended 2-2 after extra-time at Goodison Park. The replay is just as tense and equally as dramatic. Joe Fagan's Merseysiders are ahead at the break thanks to a Paul McGrath own goal, but a stunning Bryan Robson strike from distance levels things up early in the second half, and then comes the winning moment for 'Sparky' on the hour. The United half of Maine Road erupts in joy as the Welshman latches onto Gordon Strachan's through-ball to slot home, then again at the final whistle as Ron Atkinson's men secure a place in the Wembley final against Everton.

OLD TRAFFORD

The Theatre of Dreams is a home from home for all those who attend matches each season, being so much more than just a pitch with stands around it. United's home is a place packed with memories for many millions all around the world, and here's a look at its evolution…

OLD MANCHESTER UNITED IN COLOUR

Above: An aerial photograph of Old Trafford, taken while a Reserve team game is underway in March 1922, shows a small crowd in the stands.

"**The most handsomest [sic], the most spacious and the most remarkable arena I have ever seen. As a football ground it is unrivalled in the world, it is an honour to Manchester and the home of a team who can do wonders when they are so disposed**," gushed the *Sporting Chronicle*, summarising Old Trafford's first-ever fixture.

Ever since that groundbreaking afternoon when the Reds hosted Liverpool in February 1910, the home of Manchester United has been hallowed ground. Funded by chairman James W Gibson and designed by noted architect Archibald Leitch, Old Trafford provided a substantial upgrade on the club's previous home, the near-incomparable Bank Street in Clayton. The Reds had moved to Bank Street in 1893, leaving behind North Road in Newton Heath, but neither facility had an adequate playing surface, especially for a side which had won the First Division in 1908 and the FA Cup a year later, prompting Gibson to lead the search for a fitting new venue.

Leitch's body of work already included Ibrox and Hampden Park, and Old Trafford quickly became one of the highlights of the Scot's showreel, attracting universal acclaim and quickly interesting the Football Association, who located the FA Cup finals of 1911 and 1915 at United's new base. The following decade, the stadium hosted international football for the first time as England faced Scotland in M16, and a stadium-record attendance of 76,962 supporters crammed into Old Trafford to watch Wolverhampton Wanderers and Grimsby Town do battle in 1939's FA Cup semi-final.

Six months later, however, the outbreak of the Second World War halted the steep upward trajectory of the stadium's fortunes. Not only did competitive football cease, but Old Trafford twice fell foul of Luftwaffe bombings, in December 1940 and March 1941, leaving United homeless and searching for a solution for the remainder of the conflict. A compromise was eventually reached whereby, once football resumed, the Reds' home games would take place at Maine Road (rented from Manchester City), while Old Trafford was rebuilt.

While the restoration took place, United's operations ran out of an office at Cornbrook Cold Storage, a business owned by Gibson,

Above: Trainer Jack Crompton (on left) and Sir Matt Busby walk along the Old Trafford pitch in 1970, watching a Reserve match being played.

around a mile from Old Trafford. Therein, newly-appointed manager Matt Busby, club secretary Walter Crickmer and his assistant, Les Olive, set about rebuilding the club for the post-war era. Within long, they were joined by assistant manager Jimmy Murphy, who noted: "When I arrived at Old Trafford after being demobbed in 1946, I came whistling along full of the joys of spring and stopped dead in my tracks. The place looked as though it had been hit by a bomb, which in fact it had. Where once there had been a stand, there was now a pile of twisted metal."

The only way was up and, under Busby's charge, United began building for the future on a new footballing landscape. By the time Old Trafford was re-opened in 1949, the Reds were on the rise, FA Cup winners a year earlier and crowned First Division champions in 1952. Thereafter, the Scot flooded his team with talented young players, the vast majority of them homegrown, and made clear their responsibility to treat their stage with respect.

"Matt Busby talked of the duty of professional footballers to provide a little spark, a little colour, for the men and women who come to Old Trafford at the end of a working week," recalled Bobby Charlton, who later coined the stadium's famous moniker 'The Theatre of Dreams'. "They wanted something to carry them through the drab days of winter. They wanted excitement and it was a professional footballer's duty to always produce as much of that as he possibly could."

Charlton's breakthrough came in October 1956, after the Busby Babes had won their first title together, and his debut marked the start of a career so stellar that one of Old Trafford's stands would later be named in his honour. Fittingly, it was love at first sight for the gifted youngster and his new playground.

"Compared to today's Old Trafford, the

> **"I arrived at Old Trafford full of the joys of spring and stopped dead in my tracks. The place looked as though it had been hit by a bomb, which in fact it had"**
>
> – Jimmy Murphy

OLD MANCHESTER UNITED IN COLOUR

Above: Old Trafford was the place to be during the 1960s, with star players like Denis Law capturing the imagination of the fans. This image of the Scot was taken on 20 January 1968, in a league clash with Sheffield Wednesday that the Reds would win 4-2 in front of a 55,254 crowd.

pitch that welcomed me was in the middle of a football shanty town," admitted the future national treasure. "The Stretford and city [Scoreboard] ends were uncovered and the stand across from the main one would have looked to the modern eye flimsy and ramshackle. Yet as far as I was concerned it might all have been lit up by the most beautiful neon. 'Bobby, lad,' I said to myself, 'there are no two ways around it. You are now in paradise.' I believed that I would have the scene fixed in my mind forever – and so it has proved."

Charlton was part of the England squad which won the 1966 World Cup, with Old Trafford hosting three group-stage games to cap its return to splendour after its wartime downfall. In order to guarantee its suitability for the tournament, the stadium was fitted with new cantilever roofing, another upgrade following the 1957 arrival of floodlights, and thereafter the subsequent switch to all-seater format in the early 1990s continued the ground's evolution into an outstanding modern venue fit for the Reds' 25-year dominance either side of the new millennium. Change has continued apace, with benches making way for dugouts, the players' tunnel and dressing rooms shifting from the South Stand to the corner of the Stretford End, the renaming of stands after Sir Bobby and Sir Alex, and the smattering of statues around and inside the stadium: Ferguson, Charlton, Busby, George Best, Denis Law (twice) and now Jimmy Murphy, forever immortalised in bronze.

The largest club stadium in the country, second only in capacity to Wembley, has, through it all, witnessed countless acts of brilliance by an all-star cast born for the stage. All-time greats of the game have graced the United shirt and enraptured those in the stands, ensuring that, while the

"'Bobby, lad,' I said to myself, 'there are no two ways around it. You are now in paradise'"

– Bobby Charlton on arriving at Old Trafford

"It's great to have that connection with Old Trafford. Our form here has been excellent and a major part of that success has been the contribution of the fans"

– Erik ten Hag

extinction of terracing had an unavoidable impact on atmospheres at grounds around the country, the Reds' home fixtures are often soundtracked by a raucous din. From the relentless 90-minute stridence rolled out for huge fixtures and local derbies to the explosive joy of a last-gasp winner, the sound of Old Trafford in full voice is an unforgettable experience for those who sample it.

Harnessing the power of the crowd has always been a signature move of the club's most successful managers, with Ferguson and Busby the masters of promoting reciprocity between those in the stands and those on the pitch, and Erik ten Hag noted as much in his first season, which yielded a joint club record 27 home wins.

"It's great to have that connection with Old Trafford," admitted the Dutchman. "Being at Old Trafford is a huge advantage for us because we have seen repeatedly just how big a difference our fantastic home support can make. Our form here has been excellent and a major part of that success has been the contribution of the fans."

Working in tandem over the course of well over a century, players and supporters have conjured some magical, stupefying memories together at Old Trafford: truly, the Theatre of Dreams.

Below: United captain Martin Buchan shows off the Division Two trophy to the Old Trafford crowd on 26 April 1974

OLD MANCHESTER UNITED IN COLOUR

Old Trafford is a scene of devastation, and plenty of vegetation, in September 1945. The war is over and the rebuilding job can begin, although it will be another four years before the stadium is fit to host top-level football again. This photograph shows the demolition of the main stand roof, which had taken pride of place at the ground since its opening in 1910. Due to its proximity to Trafford Park, United's home had been hit by German bombs twice in the space of four months during the conflict: first in December 1940, then again in March 1941. It was the latter that did most damage, destroying the club offices, much of the main stand, and scorching the pitch.

OLD TRAFFORD

Home sweet home! Manchester United return to Old Trafford (24 August 1949) and take on Bolton Wanderers in the first competitive match at the stadium since before the Second World War. After the destruction of the main stand by German bombs in March 1941, the Reds had used Manchester City's Maine Road for home matches until the end of the 1948/49 season. There was no roof over the new main stand yet, in fact there were only three small covered sections in the whole ground, but being back home was something to celebrate. And the 41,748 crowd did just that as Matt Busby's first home match ended with a 3-0 victory for the Reds – thanks to an own goal, a Charlie Mitten penalty and a Jack Rowley header.

OLD MANCHESTER UNITED IN COLOUR

By the 1950s, Old Trafford was enjoying bumper crowds due the excitement created by Matt Busby's vibrant young side. Nicknamed the 'Babes' by the British press, the team won back-to-back league titles in 1956 and 1957. Pictured are members of that team – (left to right) Billy Whelan, Bobby Charlton, Dennis Viollet, Wilf McGuinness, Eddie Colman and David Pegg – taking to the pitch ahead of a league game. Standing close to Charlton is club mascot Jack Irons, dressed in club colours, although he doesn't appear to be carrying the red-and-white umbrella that was part of his pre-match entertainment routine. At this time the dressing rooms were situated beneath the main stand, with the players' tunnel giving them access to the field of play. That remained unchanged until 1993 when new dressing rooms and players' tunnel were introduced in the south-west corner of the stadium.

OLD TRAFFORD

Stadium expansion continued through the 1960s and beyond, with this aerial view of Old Trafford showing how the ground looked ahead of the 1966 World Cup. This photograph was taken on 30 March that year, during the Reds' FA Cup quarter-final replay against Preston North End. The game was won 3-1 thanks to goals from Denis Law (2) and John Connelly, but it's the new cantilever stand on the United Road side of the ground – complete with state-of-the-art executive boxes – that is the main focus of attention. This new phase of redevelopment was brought about for the pending international tournament, during which Old Trafford hosted three group games. A crowd of 60,433 were inside the stadium on this particular day, with the only uncovered section being the Scoreboard End (which was eventually covered in 1973).

Right: Training sessions would mainly take place at The Cliff by the 1960s, although Old Trafford would still be used on occasion – as shown in this photo. Pictured (l-r) are Denis Law, Pat Dunne, Paddy Crerand, George Best and Tony Dunne making their way around the pitch in March 1965. Behind the players is the new United Road stand slowly taking shape.

Left: Inside the United souvenir shop at Old Trafford are (left to right) Edith Rawcliffe, Nesta Burgess and Renee Loughnane, pictured on 4 April 1976. A day earlier the Reds had reached the FA Cup final, beating Derby County 2-0 at Hillsborough in the Cup semi-final.

OLD TRAFFORD

26 May 1966: United's hardworking stadium staff take time out for a photograph ahead of final preparations for the three World Cup group games to played in Manchester. Whereas today the club has almost 1,000 full-time employees, back in the mid-1960s it was down to this group of men to carry out general maintenance on the stadium and to keep the pitch in as good a condition as possible.

THE FANS

What sets Manchester United apart from most other clubs is the size, passion and devotion of its supporters – as so clearly displayed in this collection of fan-related images dating right back to the 1920s...

OLD MANCHESTER UNITED IN COLOUR

Above: FA Cup fever grips Old Trafford and these two very young fans walk away from the ground with tickets for a fifth-round home tie with Burnley in February 1965.

Seasons change, players come and go and eras bloom and inevitably fade. Football's endless mutability is one of its greatest strengths. But there is one constant – not just at Manchester United, but at every club. The fans.

Old Trafford is English football's biggest club stadium, and has been a magnificent venue ever since it opened in 1910, with a dramatic 4-3 defeat to Liverpool. At that time, United could count on strong local support, much like neighbours Manchester City, but during the course of the 20th century, the Red Army mushroomed like few other fanbases. By the 1980s, United could justifiably regard itself as one of the few European club teams with truly national and international appeal. Since the Second World War, the club has topped the attendance charts in the overwhelming majority of domestic seasons. Even during the infamous 1974/75 season when the Reds dropped into the second tier, Old Trafford's average attendance of 48,389 was comfortably clear of Division One champions Liverpool.

But the beginnings of United's support was more modest. The club's first ground, at North Road in Newton Heath, could accommodate around 12,000 fans, and was replaced by Clayton's Bank Street in 1893. The new premises were more capacious, and the first covered stand in the country was added in 1906, thanks to investment from new owner John Henry Davies.

United's first halcyon age came in the wake of Davies' involvement. The brewery owner became involved in 1902 (the same year the club was named 'Manchester United') and helped to solve some outstanding debt issues. Later in the decade, as United won a first league title, plans became advanced to build a bespoke new stadium at Old Trafford.

The emergence of the Busby Babes amped up the romantic attachment between United and our fans even further. The whole country wanted to watch Matt Busby's exciting new team and those lucky enough to live in and around Manchester were even more intoxicated by their unique spell

Designed by Archibald Leith – the architectural master behind most of British football's famous grounds – Old Trafford could house up to 80,000 supporters, and boasted a gym, a billiards room and curved terraces.

United boasted a loyal support and while fans were largely limited to attending home matches prior to the Second World War, there was the odd dramatic excursion, like the 1909 FA Cup final, when the more intrepid United fans travelled down to distant Crystal Palace. But otherwise, affordability and transport restrictions meant most supporters' best leisure option was to watch whichever nearby club was playing at home that weekend.

Lifelong United fan Pete Sharman gave us an insight into the inter-war years during a recent interview, when he presented some memories of his father. "Even though the club was nothing like it is now and had few successes," he explained, "my dad's generation were just as passionate, and they had interesting things to say [about football]. My dad once walked from Hulme to Edgeley Park, when United and Stockport were in the Second Division!"

After the Second World War, it became more common for fans to begin following their beloved team around the country. "By the late '40s, I was going regularly to watch us at Maine Road and local grounds like Bolton, Burnley, Anfield and Stoke," recalls Sharman. The emergence of the Busby Babes amped up the romantic attachment between United and our fans even further. The whole country

Below: This group of Reds are at Wembley to cheer United to FA Cup triumph in May 1983, but a 2-2 draw means they'll be back again four days later for a replay against Brighton (and a stunning 4-0 win!).

OLD MANCHESTER UNITED IN COLOUR

THE FANS

Throughout the '50s and '60s, United fans were increasingly inclined to take time out to travel and enjoy the spectacle on offer whenever and wherever. In the process, a clear community and a culture formed, which endures to this day

wanted to watch Matt Busby's exciting new team, and those lucky enough to live in and around Manchester were even more intoxicated by their unique spell.

"The first 10 or so times I went to London was for football," continues Pete. "We'd get there about five in the morning, go to Covent Garden for a beer, and then play football at Hyde Park until about half 11. Then it was something to eat, a few beers, the game, and the same after, before the coach back at midnight. There was great camaraderie, and I made so many great pals."

This was the first real flourishing of what we now know as the culture of home-and-away match-going football support. Throughout the 1950s and 1960s, as United's swashbuckling teams bewitched the country, fans were increasingly inclined to take time out to travel and enjoy the spectacle on offer whenever and wherever possible. In the process, a clear community and a culture formed, which endures to this day.

The 1970s and 1980s brought further development, and some problems too. Match-going football culture became intertwined with new fashions (the 'casual' movement) and musical subcultures (mod, punk, new wave), but outbreaks of violence and other anti-social behaviours also crept in. United fans were not completely innocent: in 1977, the Red Army was embroiled in ugly scenes during the first leg of a Cup Winners' Cup tie against Saint-Etienne. It led to the second leg being played in Plymouth, with Old Trafford and Manchester deemed too much of a risk by the relevant authorities.

Such flashpoints revealed negative aspects to passionate football support. But the upside was that United were the best-supported club in the country, backed by the famous 'Red Army' wherever we played. During the infamous season in Division Two, under Tommy Docherty, thousands descended on relatively small market towns across England, determined to demonstrate their monumental affection for the Reds.

When United qualified for the UEFA Cup in 1976, thousands of younger Reds took the opportunity to head abroad to sample a little bit of the continent's delights. Some supporters had travelled overseas before, for landmark matches like the 1968 European Cup semi-final second leg against Real Madrid, but with international travel becoming more affordable by the year, a cast of thousands made the trip to Amsterdam in '76.

Such developments also made it more achievable for foreign fans to visit Old Trafford too. Fans from Ireland and Scandinavia had grown up watching Match of the Day and FA Cup finals, and many had adopted United due to the team's romantic appeal under Busby. Throughout the 1970s and 1980s, it became more common for groups of supporters to head to Manchester to experience the magic of Old Trafford first-hand.

These decades saw the club undergo ups and downs on the pitch, but the devotion of our support never faltered. The passion came from myriad places – a romantic history, the legacy of the Busby Babes and Munich, the majesty of Old Trafford – but Manchester United's appeal was clear and consistent, long before the golden Sir Alex Ferguson era of the 1990s and 2000s kicked in.

Left: Denis Law delights these two supporters by stopping to sign autographs on the day he finally becomes a Red, in July 1962.

OLD MANCHESTER UNITED IN COLOUR

THE FANS

27 March 1926: A sea of faces (and flat caps) await the teams ahead of the all-Manchester FA Cup semi-final at Bramall Lane in Sheffield, with this section of the crowd made up of United supporters. The messages on the placard – 'Play up United' and 'Give it Joe' – were both familiar cries heard at Old Trafford, with the latter referring to Reds' attacker and big crowd favourite Joe Spence. As a reflection of football crowds in the inter-war era, this photograph paints a thousand words. Team colours were rarely worn, there's not a female to be seen and every spectator is wearing a hat of some description. But what remains unchanged to the current day is the camaraderie of the collective, the smiles on faces, the humour of the terrace, and the undoubted dedication and devotion to Manchester United Football Club.

United supporters arrive at Euston Station, London, en route to Highbury, to watch the Reds take on Arsenal in the fourth round of the FA Cup on 30 January 1937. The fan in the hat is waving a rattle, an instrument used in the First World War trenches to warn of poison gas attacks and later by air raid wardens to warn the public of impending raids during the Second World War. The clicking of the rattle would be used to generate noise in support of the team, and often decorated in the club colours, like the one in this photo. Colour ribbons and rosettes would also be worn for big matches, as demonstrated here by the two fans leaning out of the carriage window. They certainly appear excited about their day ahead as they arrive in the capital, but they were possibly more subdued on their return journey after watching United lose 0-5 to the Gunners. Ouch!

OLD MANCHESTER UNITED IN COLOUR

Up for the Cup! A group of excited United fans walk past the gates of Buckingham Palace on the morning of the FA Cup final between the Reds and Blackpool at Wembley Stadium on 24 April 1948. While winning the league championship was always deemed the more difficult achievement, Cup final day was the biggest on the English football calendar – something clearly reflected in the excitement on the faces of these Reds fans. With them is club mascot Jack Irons, second from left at the front, who is decked out in United colours including two large rosettes on the lapels of his jacket. Rosettes and ribbons were worn widely at matches, especially for Cup ties, and this group would certainly have made themselves heard; Irons has a bell in his hand, while others in the group have rattles ready to make noise for their team.

THE FANS

Ten years on from the adjacent photograph, these United fans – again led by mascot Jack Irons – are in London to watch the Reds take on Fulham in an FA Cup semi-final replay at Highbury. Jack could be seen at every home match, and in 1946 is thought to have been enrolled as the club's honorary mascot – being given a seat inside the ground and paraded around the pitch, greeting fans and signing autographs. When Real Madrid visited Old Trafford in April 1957, the club had a red and white suit made for him to go with his bowler hat and unfurled red and white umbrella emblazoned with the club name. On this particular day, 26 March 1958, these fans were part of a 38,000 crowd that watched Jimmy Murphy's newly-assembled side beat Fulham 5-3 to reach the FA Cup final against the odds.

OLD MANCHESTER UNITED IN COLOUR

THE FANS

Trafalgar Square has often been a matchday destination for fans visiting London ahead of a final, and these two Reds were determined to bring some colour and noise to the capital ahead of the 1948 FA Cup final. Wearing two scarves each, carrying bells and rattles, you can be sure that they made themselves heard at Wembley, too – especially after Matt Busby's side came from behind to beat Blackpool 4-2 in one the great FA Cup finals.

OLD MANCHESTER UNITED IN COLOUR

Here come the Reds... much to the excitement of the United fans next to the players' tunnel at Villa Park on 22 March 1958. Jimmy Murphy's briskly rebuilt XI are about to take on Fulham in the FA Cup semi-final, and the fans are decked out just as you'd expect in the late 1950s: rattles in hand, scarves around necks, with some wearing rosettes on their chests. The game ended as a 2-2 draw, with United going on to reach the Wembley final via a replay at Highbury four days later.

THE FANS

OLD MANCHESTER UNITED IN COLOUR

Right: Fans queue for tickets for the weekend's league game against Wolves, and the following week's FA Cup tie against Sheffield Wednesday, at Old Trafford late on the afternoon of 6 February 1958. News of United's plane crashing in Munich was coming through, but the severity still unknown.

Left: Matt Busby and Bobby Charlton meet young fan Leslie Ripley of Barking, East London, ahead of United's league visit to Tottenham Hotspur's White Hart Lane in January 1962.

Fans once again make their way to Trafalgar Square on FA Cup final day, this time ahead of the 1963 clash with Leicester City at Wembley. Rosettes, scarves and rattles are still all staples for these fans, with the addition of a home-made banner.

29 May 1968: Excitement builds ahead of the European Cup final at Wembley, and the United fans have a clear message for the British public. Their affection for the Reds boss is further enhanced by a 4-1 victory over Benfica on a glorious, unforgettable evening.

THE FANS

Left: There were even more banners on display in Trafalgar Square ahead of European's football showpiece fixture, with plenty of joy to come for United fans against Benfica that May evening of 1968.

Right: Matt Busby was always delighted to meet supporters and happily sign the autograph books of fans young and old, and does so here upon arriving in London for the '68 European Cup final.

OLD MANCHESTER UNITED IN COLOUR

This young, lone United supporter, who is making no effort to hide his allegiance, looks less than impressed as the Stoke City fans celebrate a goal in an FA Cup sixth-round replay at the Victoria Ground on 22 March 1972. His hero George Best did at least provide a moment to enjoy – scoring United's goal – but the Potters went on to win 2-1 in extra-time. This is the sixth of seven meetings in three competitions between United and Stoke in 1971/72, with Frank O'Farrell's side winning just one of them. As for Best, he scored four goals across those games and 26 goals in total across the campaign.

THE FANS

Left: Manchester United and Liverpool is the biggest game in English football... except someone forgot to tell this policeman when he was at this Old Trafford clash of the north-west rivals in December 1966, a thrilling 2-2 draw!

Right: United's appeal is ever increasing, with these Reds from the Channel Islands making the long trek north for the Manchester derby on 5 March 1977. They are rewarded by seeing Tommy Docherty's Reds beat Manchester City 3-1!

OLD MANCHESTER UNITED IN COLOUR

15 September 1976: Three of the over 7,000 United fans who travelled to Amsterdam, Netherlands, to watch Tommy Docherty's Reds take on Ajax in the UEFA Cup pose for the camera. The Red Army were enjoying their first European campaign in seven years, and even a 0-1 defeat in the Olympic Stadium couldn't douse their spirits. Legendary Ajax skipper Ruud Krol scored the only goal, but Doc's Reds held on to escape with just a narrow defeat. A fortnight later, United were rampant and in the club's first European home tie since May 1969 ran out 2-0 winners thanks to goals from Lou Macari and Sammy McIlroy.

OLD MANCHESTER UNITED IN COLOUR

The age of colour photography for newspapers was drawing ever closer, but this image was taken in black and white on 22 November 1986. It shows new United manager Alex Ferguson speaking to fans at Old Trafford ahead of his first home game in charge – a 1-0 victory against Queens Park Rangers thanks to a John Sivebaek free-kick. The Scotsman would eventually oversee 724 home matches as Reds boss – and 1,500 games in total – registering an incredible Old Trafford win ratio of 71.13%.

THE TEAMS

Before the Second World War, there was a dearth of images of teams playing matches – meaning that the only real access to photos of your club was posed images of individual players or team groups like these from down the decades…

OLD MANCHESTER UNITED IN COLOUR

Above: This is the Manchester United squad ahead of the 1937/38 season, the last to be played ahead of the Second World War, with manager Scott Duncan sat fifth from right on the 2nd row.

The epochal efforts of Sir Matt Busby and Sir Alex Ferguson insist that modern Manchester United teams are always judged on how they fare in the two competitions most important to the club's traditions: the league championship (now Premier League) and the European Cup (UEFA Champions League).

But, of course, Busby and Ferguson's eras comprise just two (admittedly sizeable) chunks of United history. The full story is a complicated epic, with teams of all shapes and sizes. Not all of them climbed football's highest peaks, but that's not to say many of them were not wholeheartedly loved by Manchester United fans.

The most memorable team of the pre-war period was forged by Ernest Mangnall – perhaps the third-best United manager in history – who led the Reds to two titles (1907/08, 1910/11) and a first FA Cup (1908/09) before moving across town to join Manchester City. Mangnall signed some legendary players, among them ball-playing defender and captain Charlie Roberts, plus one of the period's most famous footballers, Welsh winger Billy Meredith. Also in attack was Sandy Turnbull, whose 25 league goals fuelled the 1907/08 title drive. Turnbull then scored the winner in the 1909 FA Cup final against Bristol City, before meeting a tragic end at the Battle of Arras during the penultimate year of the First World War. It was a talented team crammed with charismatic individuals but, crucially, also a punishingly fit one. Mangnall was an early stickler for physical conditioning, and had even cycled from Land's End to John O'Groats during his younger days.

Mangnall's departure in 1912 and the outbreak of war ended the club's first golden period, and United spent much of the 1920s and 1930s oscillating between the first and second tiers of English football. In 1935/36, under Scott Duncan, United claimed the Second Division title, with George Mutch (21) and Harry Rowley (19) spearheading the forward line, but the Reds spent just one season in the top flight before sinking back down again.

The Second World War drew a firm line in the sand, and the arrival of Matt Busby in October 1945 would usher in a slew of great

THE TEAMS

FOOTBALL - MANCHESTER UNITED PLAYERS

Above: The inter-war years were turbulent times for the Reds, flitting between the top two divisions, and this is a group photo taken at Old Trafford in 1935.

United teams. The 1948 FA Cup-winning XI was one United fans of the age could recite by heart. At its centre, club captain Johnny Carey – who was named Footballer of the Year in 1949 – was famously versatile (even deputising in goal on occasion), but primarily admired for his calm leadership and classical poise on the ball. In attack, there was the trickery of Charlie Mitten on one flank, the cunning of elder statesman Jimmy Delaney on the other, with deadly finishers Jack Rowley and Stan Pearson inside, along with clever youngster Johnny Morris. They were 2-1 behind to Blackpool (and Stanley Matthews) with just 20 minutes left at Wembley, but Carey implored his teammates to "keep playing football". United duly roared back with three goals in 12 minutes, delivering a classic early template of the attacking football Busby would become famous for.

The Scot's next great team, the Busby Babes of the 1950s, afforded the club an even greater reputation for stylish, attractive play. While romping to consecutive titles in 1956 and 1957, they became a phenomenon across England, inspiring calypso records,

The most memorable team of the pre-war period was forged by Ernest Mangnall – perhaps the third-best United manager in history – who led the Reds to two titles and a first FA Cup

starstruck press encomiums and widespread teenage adulation. Their pioneering first venture into European football added to the sense of buccaneering swagger associated with the Babes, who arguably peaked with a stunning 3-0 win over Athletic Bilbao in the 1957 European Cup quarter-final second leg.

Sadly, the 1958 Munich Air Disaster brought the dream to a brutal end. But even though Busby would claim that much-coveted European Cup 10 years later (not to mention two further league titles) thanks to another great side dominated by three *Ballon d'Or* winners – George Best, Denis

OLD MANCHESTER UNITED IN COLOUR

"I have no doubt in my mind which was the greatest side, and that was the pre-Munich side. They looked as though they were going to carry everything in front of them for a few years" – Matt Busby

Below: Squad photos ahead of a new season were an annual event long before this one was taken in August 1976, prior to a campaign that would end with FA Cup triumph.

Law and Munich survivor Bobby Charlton – the great manager was convinced that the Babes' supremacy could not be topped.

"I have no doubt in my mind which was the greatest side," he told the BBC in 1973, "and that was the pre-Munich side. As even young boys, they were winning the English league championship by 11 points. Staggering, actually... staggering. They looked as though they were going to carry everything in front of them for a few years."

The next great United team might not have achieved the glories of Busby's days. But if football is about arousing passion and loyalty, Tommy Docherty's renegade band of brothers from the mid-1970s surely have few equals. The Doc technically took United down to the Second Division, but the manner in which he resuscitated the club thereafter is still discussed with an awed reverence by supporters.

Confronted with the abyss, Docherty instructed his players to go for broke, and devised a wildly attacking 4-2-4 formation to help them terrorise opponents. First, they did it in the Second Division. But incredibly, once promoted back to the big time, they continued to wreak havoc with much

THE TEAMS

Above: Matt Busby, club directors and players sit for a studio-taken photograph to celebrate winning the FA Cup in 1948.

the same effect. There was one survivor from the 1968 European Cup-winning team, goalkeeper Alex Stepney, and steely defenders in captain Martin Buchan and Jim Holton. But after that, Doc's red arrows were full of skill and pace, embodied by the tireless running of Lou Macari and the directness of wingers Steve Coppell and Gordon Hill. They came close to the Double in 1976, only to fall agonisingly short in both competitions. Never one to shy away from a bold statement, after the Reds' frustrating defeat to Southampton in the FA Cup final, Docherty simply told supporters United that they'd win the competition the next season. Typically, the Doc succeeded in pulling it off, with a 2-1 victory over eternal rivals Liverpool in 1977.

The league title might have remained elusive until Alex Ferguson hit top gear in the 1990s, but United's cup heroics would continue through the 1980s. Like Docherty's much-loved 1970s outfit, the Ron Atkinson sides of the early-to-mid 1980s were all about entertainment and charisma. In hard and skilful players like captain Bryan Robson,

Frank Stapleton and Norman Whiteside, they had personality in abundance, even if issues with injuries and consistency ultimately cost them serious tilts at the league championship.

But they regularly delivered golden days for United's ravenous supporters, most notably in the cup finals of 1983 and 1985. The '85 success over Everton, in particular – earned via an iconic Whiteside strike in extra-time – summed up the lean years between Busby and Ferguson. United might have been the unfancied club heading into the final (Everton were the new league champions), and Kevin Moran's red card (the first in FA Cup final history) left them down to 10 men for the entirety of extra-time, but talent and ticker took Big Ron's lads through.

They might not have won the game's biggest prizes, or matched the incredible standards set by some of the legendary United teams that preceded them. But they inspired huge affection from those on the terraces at Old Trafford, for regularly playing with the spirit and the style associated with Manchester United.

OLD MANCHESTER UNITED IN COLOUR

Right: Newton Heath Football Club line up in March 1895, after beating Walsall Swifts 9-0 in a replayed league game. The visitors had complain about the state of the Bank Street pitch after losing the original fixture 14-0, meaning the result was nullified. Pictured are: (back row, l-r) Alf Albut (secretary), Fred Paley (trainer), John Dow, William Douglas, Fred Palmer (director), Fred Erentz, Will Davidson, George Faulkner (director); (middle): William Crompton (president), George Perrins, James McNaught, Willie Stewart, Henry Jones (vice-president); (front): John Clarkin, Bob Donaldson, Joe Cassidy, Richard Smith and Jack Peters.

Left: Newton Heath (LYR) are Manchester & District Cup winners in 1889/90, beating Royton 5-2 in front of 4,000 fans at Brooke's Bar, in Whalley Range, Manchester.

Manchester United's first glorious era was building nicely under the guidance of manager Ernest Mangnall (above, in suit and bowler hat). The Reds narrowly missed out on promotion to the First Division in both 1903/04 and 1904/05, before finally returning to the top flight in 1905/06. In this team group photograph from the promotion campaign are: (back row, l-r): Alex Downie, Harry Moger, Bob Bonthron; (middle): Ernest Mangnall (secretary), Jack Picken, Charlie Sagar, Tommy Blackstock, Jack Peddie; (front) Clem Beddow, Charlie Roberts, Alec Bell and Tommy Arkesden.

OLD MANCHESTER UNITED IN COLOUR

Here is the Newton Heath (LYR) playing squad, wearing red and white halved shirts, ahead of the 1892/93 season – the year the Heathens joined the Football League. This photograph has often been colourised in green and yellow (or gold), which is an inaccurate interpretation seemingly based on a retro kit design brought in by kit provider Umbro in 1992. Secretary Alf Albut (pictured second from left in the middle row) and his side endured a tough introduction to life in the First Division, finishing bottom of the table. There was no automatic relegation, instead they faced a play-off against the Second Division champions, known as a Test Match. The Heathens retained their top-flight status by beating Small Heath (now known as Birmingham City) 5-2 in a replay.

THE TEAMS

OLD MANCHESTER UNITED IN COLOUR

United's home and away shirts are on display in this picture, with the photo believed to have been taken ahead of a practice match in August 1914 between the first team, reserves and triallists. Played just weeks after the outbreak of the First World War, 1914/15 was to prove a season to forget for the club. Competitive football was abandoned after this season due to public criticism, but the Reds were also embroiled in a match-fixing scandal with Liverpool on Good Friday in 1915. United won 2-0, but three players were later found guilty of conspiring, and placing bets, to fix the final result.

THE TEAMS

OLD MANCHESTER UNITED IN COLOUR

THE TEAMS

Here's United's 1907/08 squad photo, taken ahead of a practice match on 17 August 1907. These players became the club's first league title winners, led by secretary (a role that later became manager) Ernest Mangnall. Pictured are: (back, left-right): Herbert Burgess, Jimmy Bannister, William Berry, George Wall; (middle): trainer Fred Bacon, Alexander Menzies, Billy Meredith, Harry Moger, Jimmy Turnbull, Henry Mills, George Stacey, Henry Williams, Herbert Broomfield, John McGillivray, Ernest Mangnall (secretary); (front) Dick Duckworth, Edward Dalton, Jack Picken, Kerr Whiteside, Dick Holden, Ernest Thomson, Alec Bell and Sandy Turnbull. The Reds won the title by a huge nine-point margin at a time of two points for a win, inspired by captain Charlie Roberts (not in photo), winger Meredith and fired by 25-goal Sandy Turnbull.

OLD MANCHESTER UNITED IN COLOUR

THE TEAMS

Here are Manchester United's players, and manager-secretary Ernest Mangnall (first from left, back row) pictured in Chingford, Essex, ahead of the 1909 FA Cup final against Bristol City. It looks like relaxation is the order of the day, ahead of a tough but successful 90 minutes in which the Cup was brought back to Bank Street by skipper Charlie Roberts (fourth from right, front row).

OLD MANCHESTER UNITED IN COLOUR

THE TEAMS

This composite photograph was created as a souvenir for the 1908/09 FA Cup final and depicts the United secretary-manager and 14 of his players. George Livingston (spelt wrongly in the image), Alex Downie and Jack Picken were the unlucky men to miss out in the final against Bristol City, played at Crystal Palace in front of 71,401, as their team-mates secured a 1-0 victory. It was United's first FA Cup triumph and sealed by a 22nd-minute strike from Sandy Turnbull, who crashed in a rebound after Harold Halse had struck the crossbar. Although the United players are pictured in red shirts – including the goalkeeper, which was permitted by the FA at this point – both sides were requested to wear change strips for the final. So United wore a white jersey with a red 'V', plus the red rose of Lancashire on the left of the chest. Which probably explains the two roses positioned above the pen pics of the players in this image.

OLD MANCHESTER UNITED IN COLOUR

Champions again! United's players, staff and directors pose for a group photograph with the Football League First Division championship trophy, won in 1910/11. The Reds had pipped Aston Villa to the title by a single point on the final day of the campaign, securing a second championship in four seasons. It was a truly fitting way to celebrate Old Trafford's first full season (the stadium having opened in February 1910). In this photo are: (back row, l-r) Ernest Mangnall (secretary-manager), Fred Bacon (trainer), Jack Picken, Hugh Edmonds, George Murray (director), Harry Moger, John Henry Davies (chairman), Thomas Homer, George H Lawton (director), Alec Bell, William R Deakin (director): (middle): Billy Meredith, Dick Duckworth, Charlie Roberts, Sandy Turnbull, Enoch West, George Stacey; (front): Arthur Whalley, Leslie Hofton, Harold Halse and George Wall.

THE TEAMS

OLD MANCHESTER UNITED IN COLOUR

Right: 2 September 1905: United's XI for the first match of the season against Bristol City at Bank Street pose for the camera. Back (l-r): Alex Downie, Harry Moger and Robert Bonthron; middle: Ernest Mangnall, Jack Picken, Charlie Sagar, Tommy Blackstock, Jack Peddie and Fred Bacon (trainer); front: Clem Beddow, Charlie Roberts, Alec Bell and Tommy Arkesden.

Left: United's players line up ahead of a 0-0 draw at Aston Villa on 27 August 1928. They are: (back, l-r) unknown director, Jack Pullar (trainer), Ray Bennion, Bill Rawlings, Alfred Stewart, Herbert Bamlett (manager), Frank Mann, Charles Moore; (front) Jack Silcock, Joe Spence, James Hanson, Jack Wilson, William Johnston, Rees Williams, Hugh McLenahan.

THE TEAMS

Left: United's squad assemble for a photo opportunity on 2 August 1934. Scott Duncan's Second Division side would finish sixth despite George Mutch (second from left, middle row) scoring 18 league goals. The players are wearing a maroon and white hooped change kit, which was briefly adopted (and registered) as the home kit following a successful run of results from March 1934 until the end of that season. Red was quickly readopted.

Left: Here's a group photo from 1952/1953. Matt Busby's side had won the title the previous season but the boss would slowly phase out his ageing stars and bring in young players from the youth system. Pictured are: (back, l-r) Johnny Berry, Frank Clempson, John Aston, Stan Pearson, Johnny Downie and Jack Rowley; (middle) Johnny Carey, Allenby Chilton and Henry Cockburn; (front) Tommy McNulty, Reg Allen and Roger Byrne.

OLD MANCHESTER UNITED IN COLOUR

Now for a line-up with a difference… Here is a certain Matt Busby lining up for the United Services team for an exhibition match in Belfast, Northern Ireland, in 1945. Busby (back row, third from left) served as a football and fitness coach in the Army Physical Training Corps during the Second World War, and this team is made up of footballers from the British Army, Royal Navy, and Royal Air Force. Three of Busby's team-mates are among star names of the English game: Manchester City's Frank Swift (in yellow top), Blackpool's Stan Mortensen (back row, third from right), and Stoke City's Stanley Matthews (front row, first on left). Upon being released from the army, Busby would become Manchester United manager.

OLD MANCHESTER UNITED IN COLOUR

Right: United kicked off the post-War era playing at Maine Road, due to Old Trafford being bomb damaged. So here's the Reds' line-up at Maine Road to face Sunderland on 6 March 1948. On the back row are (left-to-right) Johnny Carey, John Anderson, Jack Crompton, Allenby Chilton, Henry Cockburn and John Aston. While on the front row are: Jimmy Delaney, Johnny Morris, Jack Rowley, Stan Pearson and Charlie Mitten. United won the game 3-1 with goals from Mitten, Delaney and Rowley.

Left: United's Football League First Division championship and Charity Shield winners pose with the trophies ahead of the 1952/53 season, joined by the coaches and club directors. Back row (l-r): trainer Tom Curry, club secretary Walter Crickmer, directors Alan Gibson, Dr William MacLean, Mr George Whittaker and W Petherbridge, and manager Matt Busby; (middle): Johnny Downie, Jack Rowley, John Aston, Reg Allen, Allenby Chilton, Roger Byrne, Stan Pearson; (front): Johnny Berry, Johnny Carey, Henry Cockburn and Tom McNulty.

THE TEAMS

The silverware haul is the same as in the photo from 1952, but the playing staff has changed considerably in the four years since the photo on the left was taken. In the above image – taken in September 1956 – only Roger Byrne and Johnny Berry remain from the side that had previously landed both the league championship and Charity Shield, as the Busby Babes emerge from the youth ranks to take the English game by storm. Even more players would make the step up and the Reds would retain their league title in 1957. Pictured are (back, l-r): Eddie Colman, Wilf McGuinness, Colin Webster, Ray Wood, David Pegg, Dennis Viollet and Johnny Berry; (middle): trainer Tom Curry, Jackie Blanchflower, Tommy Taylor, Freddie Goodwin, Mark Jones, Duncan Edwards, Billy Whelan, Bill Foulkes, manager Matt Busby; (front) secretary Walter Crickmer, director George Whittaker, chairman Harold Hardman, Roger Byrne, directors W Petherbridge and Alan Gibson.

OLD MANCHESTER UNITED IN COLOUR

THE TEAMS

Such was the interest in the FA Cup final back in the 1950s that photo sessions would take place in the days leading up to the Wembley showpiece fixture. Here's one such example, with members of Matt Busby's squad modelling the away shirt the Reds (whites?) would be wearing against Aston Villa on 4 May 1957. There are only 10 players pictured with trainer Tom Curry and Matt Busby, only nine of which would feature in the final – Mark Jones missing out. Villa lifted the Cup with a 2-1 win, denying the Babes the 'Double' of league and Cup. Pictured on the back row are Curry, Duncan Edwards, Jones, Ray Wood, Bobby Charlton, Bill Foulkes, and Busby. While seated are Johnny Berry, Liam Whelan, Roger Byrne, David Pegg and Eddie Colman. On the breast of the kit is the Manchester coat of arms, with it being a source of great pride to the city whenever United or City reached Wembley.

OLD MANCHESTER UNITED IN COLOUR

Right: United are lined up for a European tie at Home Park, Plymouth on 5 October 1977. UEFA ordered the Reds to play 200km from Old Trafford after crowd trouble in the first leg of our Cup Winners' Cup tie at St Etienne, France. From left to right are Brian Greenhoff, Jimmy Greenhoff, Gordon Hill, Steve Coppell, Lou Macari, Stuart Pearson, Arthur Albiston, Jimmy Nicholl, Sammy McIlroy, Alex Stepney and captain Martin Buchan. United won 2-0 (3-1 on aggregate).

Above: The rebuild begins at Old Trafford as Matt Busby, his staff and the players assemble ahead of the 1958/59 season. Eight players had been lost in the Munich Air Disaster, decimating the starting XI, but now these footballers above are determined to take the club back to the top. While they didn't quite achieve it, finishing second to Wolves in the First Division was in itself seen as a hugely impressive effort given the tragic events of the previous season.

THE TEAMS

After the loss of the Babes in Munich, it took five years for the Reds to win a trophy, landing the FA Cup in 1963, That provided a renewed belief for the club, and this is the squad in 1963/64. They are: (back row, left-right): Matt Busby (manager), Noel Cantwell, David Sadler, Bill Foulkes, Shay Brennan, David Herd, Harry Gregg, David Gaskell, Graham Moore, Maurice Setters, Pat Crerand, Jimmy Murphy (assistant manager); (front row) Bobby Charlton, Ian Moir, Albert Quixall, John Connelly, Nobby Stiles, George Best, Tony Dunne, Denis Law. Many of these players would go on to be crowned champions of England twice and European champions within the next five years.

OLD MANCHESTER UNITED IN COLOUR

Legends reunited. The 1968 European Cup-winning side are back together again in August 1975, to take part in Mike Summerbee's Testimonial match against Manchester City on 2 September 1975. Pictured are (l-r): Nobby Stiles, Tony Dunne, Bill Foulkes, George Best, Shay Brennan, Paddy Crerand (Alex Stepney is sat in front of him), Willie Morgan, Leighton James (guesting from Burnley), Bobby Charlton and Tony Book (guesting from City). The game was very entertaining, with United's European Cup-winning XI beating a City XI 4-3 thanks to goals from Morgan, Crerand, Charlton and Best.

THE TEAMS

30 July 1975: Photographers focus their lenses on Tommy Docherty's United players ahead of their return to the First Division. The Reds had romped back into the top flight in 1974/75 and there was much interest in how they would fare with their thrilling, swashbuckling approach back at English football's top table. The answer would be a pleasing one for the Red Army legions, who watched their side finish third in the league and reach the FA Cup final. Sadly, Southampton sprung a shock 1-0 victory at Wembley, but the passion and devotion for the Reds was undiminished and 12 months later they'd be back at Wembley to watch Doc's Reds lift the FA Cup and deny Liverpool the Treble.

THE PLAYERS

United have been fortunate enough to have had not just great teams but many iconic footballers pulling on the red shirt over the decades – many of whom feature within this fascinating collection of photographs...

OLD MANCHESTER UNITED IN COLOUR

Above: These two stalwarts of the Newton Heath era, Wales internationals (and brothers) Jack and Roger Doughty, are pictured long after their Heathen days, circa 1910.

A glance at United's all-time charts for leading appearance-makers and goalscorers quickly throws up familiar names; Wayne Rooney, Ryan Giggs, Paul Scholes, Gary Neville and David De Gea are all fresh in the memory of most United supporters, if not all as players then at least in some contemporary capacity as managers or pundits.

There's even a strong chance that the names of George Best, Bobby Charlton and Denis Law ring bells with younger members of United's fanbase, most likely as the trio immortalised in Old Trafford's forecourt statue. Denis Irwin, despite playing for the club in the 21st century, is known now as a club ambassador, while former teammate Mark Hughes is possibly more a recurring opposition boss than an ex-Red spearhead.

Amidst these figures of greater renown, however, are more modest names. Bill Foulkes, Alex Stepney, Tony Dunne, Jack Rowley, Dennis Viollet and Joe Spence are all among the club's leading appearance-makers, goalscorers or both, yet finding a variety of footage of them in action is nigh-on unheard of. Outside the memories of those who saw them play, their epic careers have been consolidated into a handful of still images, usually in monochrome.

In today's world, it's virtually impossible for a player to reach even the cusp of United's first team without deafening social media buzz surrounding their prospects. Quite what the carriage workers of the Lancashire and Yorkshire Railway would have made of their successors' footballing environment will never be known, but the attention on United players has been growing ever since the days of Newton Heath.

In the early 20th century, captains Charlie Roberts and Frank Barson built reputations which preceded them; Roberts as a skilled player whose efforts to unionise

THE PLAYERS

otball earned him added notoriety; Barson as one of the ame's first truly ferocious competitors with the scars (on hers) to prove it. True celebrity arrived at Old Trafford for he first time with the 1906 arrival of Billy Meredith. The inger's skill, athleticism and dedication to entertainment aptivated onlookers and also prompted cartoonists of the me to immortalise the toothpick-chewing Welshman, at time when United began winning major honours under anager Ernest Mangnall.

Two World Wars sandwiched yo-yoing fortunes and nancial strain for the Reds, but the appointment of Matt usby in 1945 prompted an upturn in fortunes and style at ld Trafford. One of the Scot's first moves was to bring Joe pence back to the club. Having notched 168 goals in 510 utings between the wars, Throckley-born Spence was a ost legend of the club, having excelled despite United's ollective shortcomings.

As part of the staff charged with coaching and scouting, pence was in a backroom setup designed to coax the est from not only established stars of the game like kipper Johnny Carey, Charlie Mitten and goal machine ck 'Gunner' Rowley, but also the new talents emerging om the youth development system bearing fruit under usby's watchful eye.

"You could not put a price on Bill [Foulkes] because you cannot buy the type of loyalty he has given Manchester United" – Jimmy Murphy

Among the group who would become known worldwide as the Busby Babes were players of varying types and attributes. "A strong and strong-headed young man who became one of the game's great captains," was Busby's summary of Roger Byrne, while assistant manager Jimmy Murphy said of Bill Foulkes: "You could not put a price on Bill because you cannot buy the type of loyalty he has given to Manchester United." Scout Joe Armstrong foretold Eddie Colman's dazzling wing play by quipping in his report: "Put a grass skirt on him, and you've got a hula hula dancer."

Scoring machines Tommy Taylor and Dennis Viollet took countless headlines and plaudits as United captured growing imaginations around the country, but it was Duncan Edwards, a footballing monolith capable of

Below: This striking image was taken of the great Bobby Charlton, one of club's longest serving players, in a game against West Ham United at Old Trafford on 6 January 1968.

OLD MANCHESTER UNITED IN COLOUR

playing in virtually any position, who became the emblem of the Babes before tragically losing his life after the Munich Air Disaster.

"At 15, he looked like a man. He played like a man," recalled Busby, years later. "Duncan Edwards was then, and has always remained to me, incomparable. His death after the Munich crash, when he was only 21 but with 18 caps already, was as far as football is concerned the biggest single tragedy that has happened to England and to Manchester United. He seemed indestructible." Jimmy Murphy also noted: "Duncan was the one player who had the lot. The one man around whom, had he survived, we could have rebuilt the Manchester United side so much more easily."

Instead, the rebuilding process – which unfolded with unprecedented attention turned the way of Old Trafford – had to lean on survivors like Foulkes, Charlton, Viollet and heroic goalkeeper Harry Gregg. Over years, their brilliance was augmented by new homegrown talents and canny recruitment, with the likes of midfielder Paddy Crerand and stopper Alex Stepney. As the Reds slowly returned to splendour, the stars of the show were three varied but untouchable talents who became known as the United Trinity: Charlton, George Best and Denis Law.

> "At 15, he looked like a man. He played like a man. Duncan Edwards was then, and has always remained to me, incomparable" – Matt Busby

"Going back to the 1960s, there was hardly any coverage of football at all," recalled Stepney, a 1966 capture from Chelsea. "If you didn't go to watch United on Saturday, you might be lucky to catch 20 minutes of highlights of their games each month. Even so, everybody knew about the Trinity. The newspapers told you how good they were. The headlines they inspired, the language that was used about them, you could tell they were special. I found that to be true when I joined United. Unfortunately, there's not a lot of film of them in action – you tend to see the same clips over and over – so if you were fortunate enough to see them then you have to make sure you cherish the memories and always remember them. I know I always will."

Below: Denis Law is interviewed outside Old Trafford by a radio journalist, with Matt Busby listening in, after signing for United in July 1962.

THE PLAYERS

"If you didn't go to watch United on Saturday, you might be lucky to catch 20 minutes of highlights of their games each month. Even so, everybody knew about the Trinity. You could tell they were special. I found that to be true when I joined United" – Alex Stepney

Charlton's blockbuster shooting, Law's penalty area prowess and Best's blood-twisting brilliance are forever enshrined on the Old Trafford forecourt for all visitors to see. As repeated champions of England and the country's first European Cup winners, the Trinity have the medals (and a *Ballon d'Or* each) to back-up their reputations.

There are, of course, countless others who have excelled for the Reds between the Trinity's individual retirements and collective commemoration. In the 1970s, supporters latched on to charismatic figures like Gordon Hill, Steve Coppell and Martin Buchan, while the combative spirit of Norman Whiteside, Mark Hughes and skipper Bryan Robson dominated much of the following decade as United marched towards the Premier League era.

Above: George Best became one of the most photographed men around in the 1960s (and beyond), with previously unseen levels of interest in a footballer – here he is in 1968.

Alex Ferguson's arrival at Old Trafford steadily coincided with the return of silverware after the comparatively barren post-Busby decades, and it took a typically United blend of charismatic recruits (Eric Cantona and Peter Schmeichel, for instance) and homegrown tyros like Giggs, Scholes, David Beckham, Nicky Butt and the Neville brothers to bed down the Reds' dominance of the era.

The late 20th century heroes onwards are all there to behold, perfectly preserved in digital video and image archives, but their forebears must also be remembered. From carriage workers to *Ballon d'Or* winners, the full spectrum of footballers have plied their trade in United's colours; the greatest story in football played out by a rich and varied ensemble.

OLD MANCHESTER UNITED IN COLOUR

Above: United captain Charlie Roberts displays medals and caps won during his impressive career in 1908 – he'd go on to play 302 games for the Reds, scoring 23 goals.

Above: Here's another star of United's first great team, with Billy Meredith - pictured playing against Queens Park Rangers in the 1908 Charity Shield – every bit as influential as Roberts (above left).

Right: United's Sandy Turnbull (on the right) and Enoch 'Knocker' West are photographed playing cricket with a broom handle at Old Trafford in 1911. Turnbull and West forged a lethal partnership in attack in 1910/11, as Ernest Mangnall's side pipped Aston Villa to the Football League championship by a point – the pair contributing 37 league goals between them, with West netting 19 times, Turnbull 18.

THE PLAYERS

Billy Meredith is widely regarded as United's first superstar, having joined from Manchester City in 1906. The Welsh international, hailing from Chirk in Denbighshire, was a tricky winger and a real character – often playing with a toothpick hanging from the corner of his mouth. Although autographed in 1911, this photograph of Meredith was taken in 1908 and shows him with his many Wales caps and the trophies won across his playing career with Chirk, City and United. His time with the Reds ended in 1921, with Billy having made 335 appearances, scoring 36 goals. Meredith still holds the record as the oldest player to represent the Reds – doing so aged 46 years and 281 days (v Derby County, on 7 May 1921).

OLD MANCHESTER UNITED IN COLOUR

Charlie Roberts is pictured (below) wearing United's change strip ahead of an away match against Arsenal at the Manor Ground, 2 September 1912. The Darlington-born deep-lying midfielder is in his final season at the club – joining Oldham Athletic in August 1913 – bringing to an end his eight years as club captain. With him as skipper, the Reds won five trophies: two Football League championships, the FA Cup and two Charity Shields. But it's not only his on-field enforcement for which Roberts remains renowned; he is also a pioneer of the Players' Union, helping set up the organisation (now the Professional Footballers' Association) with team-mate Billy Meredith. When the Football Association withdraws its recognition of the organisation in 1909, players are ordered to resign from the union – something most do to protect their livelihood. However, Roberts and the whole United side famously refuse – instead forming their own team dubbed 'The Outcasts FC' while suspended by the club. Eventually a compromise is found and Roberts' impressive Reds career is able to resume.

THE PLAYERS

Left: Here's goalkeeper Harry Moger, the final line of defence for the Reds' first major trophy-winning team. Signed from Southampton, he made 266 appearances between 1903-1912, winning two Football League titles, the FA Cup and Charity Shield with Ernest Mangnall's impressive side.

Right: 5 February 1936 – Half-back George Vose and forward Harry Rowley pose for a photograph ahead of United taking on Tottenham Hotspur at White Hart Lane, London. The game ended 0-0.

OLD MANCHESTER UNITED IN COLOUR

Right: Frank Mann joined the Reds aged 32 in March 1923 but still went on to make 197 appearances over the next eight seasons. Here, he's pictured at the Boleyn Ground on 28 September 1929, ahead of a 1-2 defeat to West Ham United.

Left: This image is taken at the same game at the Boleyn Ground, with Mann's team-mate Jack Wilson looking down the lens ahead of taking on West Ham. He played 140 games for United between 1926 and 1932.

THE PLAYERS

He only played 27 matches for United across two seasons (1936/37 and 1937/38), but Oldham-born Walter Winterbottom is a notable character within the English game. Although a cultured centre-half, his playing career was cut short by a back injury and the outbreak of the Second World War, leading him down the path of PE instructor then football coaching. He became England's first manager in 1946 and held the role until 1962, making him the Three Lions' longest-serving boss. During that period he led the national team to four successive World Cups, between 1950-1962, losing only 28 of his 139 games in charge.

OLD MANCHESTER UNITED IN COLOUR

30 October 1926: Pictured above is Joe Spence, one of Manchester United's all-time leading appearance-makers with 510 matches (1919-1933). Spence scored 168 goals and was the star of the Reds' inter-War years, with "Give it Joe!" a familiar shout from the Old Trafford crowd who loved his ability to produce a goal when the team needed it most. Here, Spence is posing for a photo ahead of an away match against West Ham – which sadly ended as a 0-4 defeat. But while this game won't feature as a highlight of his impressive Reds career, there are plenty of other times that the forward born in the North East of England could look back on with pride. Spence remains 11th on the Reds' all-time list, and although he missed out on major silverware at Old Trafford, he did win two caps for his country in 1926 (scoring once).

THE PLAYERS

This photograph shows the football team of the 70th Infantry Brigade, taken on 14 June 1941. The side comprises (third from right) Allenby Chilton, a young player at United who had moved to Old Trafford from Liverpool, making his debut in the final First Division fixture before the Second World War ended the 1939/40 season after just three games. Those matches were expunged from the records, meaning it would not be until January 1946 that Chilton – who was wounded twice in the D-Day landings – made his competitive debut (v Accrington Stanley in the FA Cup). He was 28 at the time of this first match, but still managed to play 391 times for the Reds, winning the FA Cup in 1948 and the First Division in 1952. He also won two caps for England.

Matt Busby shares his football philosophy with members of his first United team ahead of the 1946/47 season. The players have been assembled for a photocall, with the Reds boss talking to (left to right) Henry Cockburn, captain Johnny Carey, Johnny Morris and Charlie Mitten. Cockburn had signed for the Reds during the Second World War and would go on to make 275 appearances for United. Carey had represented the club prior to the global conflict, and would skipper the Reds to the FA Cup (1948) and First Division title (1952). Attackers Morris and Mitten would be part of the Cup triumph – making 93 and 162 appearances respectively.

THE PLAYERS

OLD MANCHESTER UNITED IN COLOUR

Here are four United legends, and an unidentified youngster, watching a training session in August 1954 (left to right): Duncan Edwards, Dennis Viollet, Jack Rowley and Bill Foulkes. The third of those players was about to embark on his final campaign for the Reds, leaving Old Trafford in February 1955 to become player-manager of Plymouth Argyle. But what a career Rowley had at United, playing 424 games and scoring 211 goals – stats made all the more impressive given that six years of his career were wiped out by the Second World War. By the time he departed the Reds, his young team-mates were already making an impression and in 1955/56 were champions of England (just as Rowley had been in 1952) once again.

THE PLAYERS

Below: Roger Byrne, shown here leading out his team circa 1956, is regarded as one of United's finest ever captains. He made 280 appearances for the Reds, scoring 20 goals, and was Matt Busby's chosen man to lead his young side in the mid-1950s. As skipper he led the Babes to two Football League titles and two Charity Shields, before sadly losing his life in Munich aged just 28 with some of his best years still ahead.

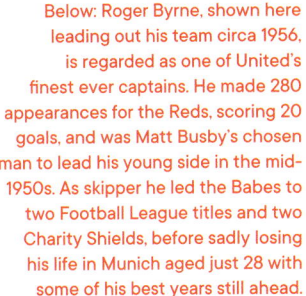

OLD MANCHESTER UNITED IN COLOUR

Duncan Edwards

Some Manchester United footballers have transcended being merely a player for the club, some have come to be regarded as icons of the game. One of those, despite losing his life aged just 21, is Duncan Edwards. "I felt I could compare with any player – except Duncan," said Sir Bobby Charlton of his friend and team-mate. "Duncan Edwards is the one person I felt inferior to. I've never known anyone so gifted, so strong and with such a presence." Edwards is pictured here signing a new contract in 1957, with his manager Matt Busby going through some of the finer details.

THE PLAYERS

4 April 1953: Jimmy Murphy congratulates 16-year-old Duncan, after making his debut for United against Cardiff City at Old Trafford. The Reds had lost the game 1-4, but this was a first glimpse of the exciting talent that was to come. At the time of his untimely death from injuries sustained in the Munich Air Disaster he was aged just 21, having played 177 times for United, scoring 21 goals. He was already viewed as one of the game's biggest talents, and his potential seemed limitless.

OLD MANCHESTER UNITED IN COLOUR

Bobby Charlton

10 June 1953: Cissie Charlton plays football with three of her sons (left to right) Gordon (10), Bobby (15), and Tommy (7) outside their home in Ashington, Northumberland. Bobby and his brother Jack, who is not pictured here, would go on to win the World Cup with England 13 years later.

THE PLAYERS

This photograph was taken on the same day as the one on the left, with schoolboy Bobby helping out with some household chores. He would become another of those falling into the 'icon' category, being rightly compared to many of the football's greatest ever players. At this point in summer 1953, Charlton had already been spotted by United's chief scout Joe Armstrong and signed on as an amateur. He'd win three consecutive FA Youth Cups with the Reds – in 1953/54, 1954/55 and 1955/56 – and then make his debut for Matt Busby's first team on 6 October 1956, scoring twice in a 4-2 victory against (fittingly) Charlton Athletic. Later that season he'd win the first of his three Football League titles with United, in April 1957.

OLD MANCHESTER UNITED IN COLOUR

Charlton is pictured with his mum Cissie again, this time in February 1958 following his discharge from hospital in Munich. Eight of his friends had been killed in the air crash, including Duncan Edwards while he was recuperating in Ashington, and such was the impact on him that he considered quitting the game. However, thanks to the encouragement of his mother, and after a number of letters from stand-in Reds boss Jimmy Murphy, Bobby decided to resume what would become a wonderful career.

THE PLAYERS

Right: Charlton takes a look at a gift from a magazine, presented to him by his manager Matt Busby, in December 1964. He's pictured with Nobby Stiles, Paddy Crerand, George Best and Denis Law.

Left: It's all eyes on Bobby as he is presented with the *Ballon d'Or* for 1966, becoming the second United player to win the award after Denis Law was voted Europe's finest player in 1964.

OLD MANCHESTER UNITED IN COLOUR

THE PLAYERS

Bobby Charlton shows off the *Ballon d'Or* trophy for 1966 after being chosen by sports writers across UEFA countries as the best player in Europe, pipping Benfica and Portugal's Eusebio to the award. His club form had been impressive enough, but his contribution to England's World Cup triumph elevated him to the top of the game. He is one of five England players nominated that year, along with Bobby Moore, Alan Ball, Gordon Banks and Geoff Hurst. He is also joined on the list of nominated players by fellow Reds Tony Dunne and Denis Law. The presentation is made to him on 18 March 1967, ahead of the Reds' home clash with Leicester City which ends in a 5-2 victory – Charlton scoring United's second goal.

OLD MANCHESTER UNITED IN COLOUR

THE PLAYERS

Here's Bobby Charlton sat with his 100 England caps a few days after bringing up the international appearance milestone against Northern Ireland at Wembley on 21 April 1970. It truly was a night to remember for the United man; Bobby Moore giving up the captain's armband for England's no.9 to wear and Charlton scoring the third goal in a 3-1 victory, as he became only the second man to reach a century of Three Lions caps (joining Billy Wright). Bobby would go on to add six more caps for his country and remains seventh on the list for all-time England appearances. The highlight, of course, being that World Cup triumph in July 1966.

OLD MANCHESTER UNITED IN COLOUR

Charlton is honoured with a CBE in the New Year honours list for 1974, and is pictured here with tennis player Virginia Wade and her MBE. The sporting pair leave Buckingham Palace on that February day after being presented with their badges by the Queen Mother. Bobby is later knighted, in 1994, for his services to football.

THE PLAYERS

The curtain falls on a wonderful career, as Charlton takes the applause of the Stamford Bridge crowd in his final competitive fixture for Manchester United. This 758th and final game for the Reds, played on 28 April 1973, ends in a 0-1 defeat – but this afternoon is all about one man. *Match of the Day* send their cameras to cover the occasion, which commences with Chelsea chairman Brian Mears presenting the United and England legend with a commemorative cigarette case. He'd play one more game for United in the Anglo-Italian Cup, scoring in a 4-1 victory over Verona, but with that game not classed as a competitive fixture, his final total stands at: 758 matches, 249 goals.

OLD MANCHESTER UNITED IN COLOUR

Right: David Pegg, aged 17, is pictured at the Hawthorns on 2 September 1953, as United take on West Bromwich Albion in a First Division fixture. He'd played 24 matches for the Reds by this point and would go on to make 150 appearances by the time of his tragic death in the Munich Air Disaster in 1958.

Left: 20 February 1962: United players (l-r) Johnny Giles, Nobby Lawton, Nobby Stiles and Shay Brennan relax in their Blackpool hotel ahead of an FA Cup tie at Sheffield Wednesday the next day.

THE PLAYERS

Left: Nobby Stiles and David Sadler are pictured at Old Trafford in the mid-1960s. The pair are part of the side that would win the European Cup in 1968.

Right: Here's one of the more unusual images from the United archives, showing Brian Kidd and boxing legend Muhammad Ali squaring up for the cameras in the early 1970s.

OLD MANCHESTER UNITED IN COLOUR

Denis Law

All hail the new king! Denis Law finally signs for Manchester United at Old Trafford on 12 July 1962, after moving from Torino to the Reds for a British record transfer of £115,000. The Aberdonian's career had taken him to Italy via Huddersfield Town and Manchester City, but after a difficult year in Turin he was keen to return to the UK. Pictured with Law at his signing are (l-r): agent Gigi Peronace, Matt Busby, Jimmy Murphy and club secretary Les Olive.

THE PLAYERS

Just over a month later and Law is ready to play his first competitive match for the Reds, with this photo taken a day before his debut against West Bromwich Albion on 18 August 1962. The striker is given the no.10 shirt – presented to him (above) by manager Matt Busby – and scores after just seven minutes of his debut, played in front of 51,685 at Old Trafford. That early goal was netted just six minutes after David Herd had put the Reds 1-0 up against the Baggies in the first minute, but sadly the visitors fought back to grab two goals in the final 15 minutes for a 2-2 draw. However, he'd end his first season with 29 goals from 44 appearances.

OLD MANCHESTER UNITED IN COLOUR

THE PLAYERS

Here's a sight to strike fear into any 1960s goalkeeper! Denis Law fires the ball right down the lens of a camera in a pre-season training session at Old Trafford on 23 August 1963. The following day the Reds play out a 3-3 draw with Sheffield Wednesday at Hillsborough, fighting back from falling 0-2 down to claim a point. Law is not among the goals, but that proves an anomaly in the 1963/64 season, which proves to be the most prolific of the Scotsman's career. He scores a still club-record 46 goals in 42 Reds appearances in all competitions, and is duly rewarded for his efforts by being named European Footballer of the Year for 1964.

Worth the wait! Here's Law picking up his *Ballon d'Or* on 19 May 1965, having been voted Europe's finest footballer for the previous calendar year. He wins the award ahead of Luis Suarez of Inter Milan (second place), Amancio of Real Madrid (in third), and Eusebio of Benfica (fourth). In addition to his 46 goals from 42 matches in 1963/64, he nets 49 United goals in the calendar year 1964, and ends his Reds career with 237 goals from 404 matches between 1962 and 1973.

THE PLAYERS

Left: 19 April 1965: Law shares a joke with a cameraman at St Andrews, as a United team beat Birmingham City 4-2 to move closer to the league title.

Left: Law poses with the lid of the FA Cup on his head in the Wembley dressing room after the Reds have beaten Leicester 3-1 on 25 May 1963. Law, who scores United's opener, sits between team-mates David Herd (left) and Maurice Setters.

OLD MANCHESTER UNITED IN COLOUR

George Best

THE PLAYERS

Left: Here's the third of the United Trinity, George Best, celebrating after scoring against Manchester City for the Reds' youth team in an FA Youth Cup semi-final second leg at Maine Road in April 1964. Best had slid in attempting to score only for City's Mike Doyle to put the ball into his own net. It helped secure an 8-4 aggregate win for the Reds, who went on to lift the Youth Cup, and years later Best would describe this photograph as one of the favourites from his career. "A chance came and I steamed in hard," he recalled. "Mike Doyle slid in with me and the ball went skidding in off his foot. This great shot ended up in the *Manchester Evening News*. It shows the ball in the net and me leaning on a post, laughing!"

Best gets into his car outside his home in Bramhall, Cheshire, circa 1970. He was by this point one of the most famous people in the country, his every move followed by the UK media.

George Best stops to sign autographs for excited young United fans after the Reds' First Division fixture against Aston Villa on 6 April 1964. Best is the rising star of Matt Busby's emerging side, making a real impact in his debut first-team season. The winger ends 1963/64 with six goals from 26 matches, and also wins an FA Youth Cup winners' plaque.

OLD MANCHESTER UNITED IN COLOUR

Best at London Airport wearing a souvenir sombrero after arriving from Lisbon, Portugal, having catapulted himself into the consciousness of world football in March 1966. In Britain he was already regarded as the finest player around, despite being only a teenager with barely two seasons of senior football behind him. Now, after blitzing Benfica in Estadio da Luz – scoring twice in the opening 13 minutes of a stunning 5-1 European Cup quarter-final win – he was to move from match reports on the back page to the focus on the front. In Portugal they labelled him 'El Beatle', in the UK 'the fifth Beatle', as his appearance drew comparisons to the band dominating world music. "I was 19 or 20 when The Beatles were at their peak and I was coming up to the peak of my career, too. I was also the first footballer to have long hair and that's how I got my nickname 'the Fifth Beatle'," recalled Best some years later. It was an iconic moment that changed his life forever.

THE PLAYERS

OLD MANCHESTER UNITED IN COLOUR

Best is joined by Alex Stepney at a photocall at Old Trafford on 25 July 1968, just weeks after the two players helped United to finally win the European Cup. Stepney had ensured normal time ended level at 1-1 with crucial late saves, with Best then putting the Reds 2-1 up two minutes into extra-time. Brian Kidd and Bobby Charlton then rounded off the scoring, Charlton getting his second, as Benfica were vanquished 4-1 in the Wembley final.

THE PLAYERS

Best shows off his close control for the cameras at The Cliff training ground in August 1970. He's still at the peak of his powers – winning the *Ballon d'Or* in 1968 – but Sir Matt Busby has retired and United's place at the top of the game is beginning to slip away. By the end of his time at Old Trafford, his contract being cancelled in June 1974, George had played 470 matches and scored 179 goals.

OLD MANCHESTER UNITED IN COLOUR

George Best often described United manager Sir Matt Busby as a father figure, and here the two men are pictured together ahead of an FA hearing in 1971. The Northern Irishman had picked up a number of bookings across the season and was requested to attend an FA disciplinary committee – Sir Matt attending with him after returning to the manager's role for the latter half of 1970/71. There was great affection between the two, with Sir Matt a huge admirer of Best's talent, once saying: "He was able to use either foot – sometimes he seemed to have six!"

OLD MANCHESTER UNITED IN COLOUR

Such was Best's fame that business opportunities presented themselves away from the football pitch, like his 'Edwardia' fashion boutique in Manchester. Here, he's pictured outside his shop with pop star Don Fardon on 19 March 1970. That month, the singer released an ode to Best entitled 'Belfast Boy', which would feature in a BBC documentary of the same year entitled *The World of Georgie Best*.

THE PLAYERS

From the moment he decimated Benfica's defence to help United become the first team in European competition to win in Estadio da Luz in 1966, the media attention surrounding 'the fifth Beatle' was immense. He was suddenly not just a great footballer, one of the finest on the planet at that, but he was now an idol to millions whether they followed the game or not. This photograph from 25 July 1968 shows him in the limelight once again, being the Football Writers' Association Player of the Year (1967/68), a European champion, and soon to be European Footballer of the Year (for 1968). He ended his career with two Football League titles, one European Cup and two Charity Shields. Many still regard Best as the greatest player ever to represent the club.

OLD MANCHESTER UNITED IN COLOUR

Much attention is given to the United Trinity and rightly so, but the guile of those three immensely gifted footballers would not have been so ably expressed but for the grit of those around them. And when it came to grit there have been fewer in Reds history to match Nobby Stiles. The midfielder was a key cog in Busby's wonderful 1960s side and equally integral to England's World Cup win in 1966. He gave every ounce of effort in his 395 matches for the Reds (and 28 games for his country), and here he's pictured ahead of a league game at Chelsea on 9 January 1971.

THE PLAYERS

Two of United's greatest ever goalkeepers share a lighter moment in the gym at Old Trafford in 1978. Harry Gregg, who played 247 times for the Reds, was the club's goalkeeping coach under manager Dave Sexton and here he shares a joke with United's new goalkeeping recruit from South Africa, Gary Bailey. The latter would eventually replace Alex Stepney in goal and make 375 appearances for the Reds, not to mention play for England, and he later said of Gregg's support: "I really loved him as a coach and spending one-on-one time with him, and receiving the advice and guidance he offered was invaluable. Goalkeepers are a separate breed and Harry was brilliant for me. As a young player, I had a lot of things going through my head so to have that connection with him was fantastic." Bailey would go on to win two FA Cups (in 1983 and 1985) and the Charity Shield (1983) with United.

OLD MANCHESTER UNITED IN COLOUR

24 May 1963: United players Tony Dunne, Pat Crerand, Harry Gregg and Noel Cantwell are part of the Reds party visiting Shaftesbury Theatre on the eve of the FA Cup final versus Leicester City. They'd lift the Cup the next day with a 3-1 victory.

THE PLAYERS

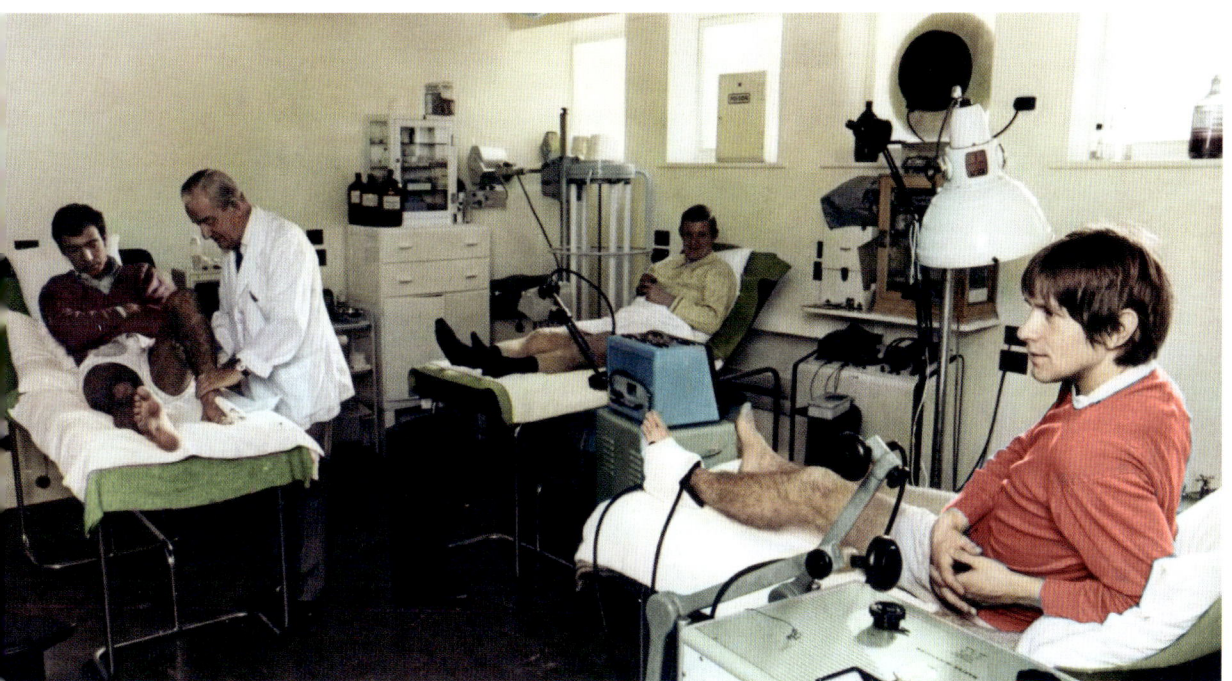

Above: United's physiotherapist Ted Dalton checks out the injury status of David Sadler, with Bobby Noble and John Fitzpatrick also undergoing treatment. This photo, taken in the medical room at The Cliff training ground, is from 14 October 1968.

Modern day fitness and training methods have changed considerably since the 1960s, but the one thing that hasn't is the demand for sweat and toil. Here, at The Cliff training ground, Brian Kidd and Alex Stepney are put through a pre-season weights session by coaches John Aston Snr (on the right) and Jack Crompton (seated). Watching on are John Aston Jnr and Shay Brennan, who look a little concerned about the bench balanced on breezeblocks – or possibly the rather random hammer placed next to Crompton!

26 February 1986: Reds striker Mark Hughes poses with his new sports car outside of his home in Bowden, Cheshire. The Welshman has emerged as one of the game's most exciting forwards and is due to move to Barcelona that summer. Sparky, as he was nicknamed, leaves the Reds after playing 118 matches and scoring 47 goals. However, two years later he is back at Old Trafford – rejoining Alex Ferguson's Reds after a difficult spell at the Nou Camp, but a promising loan period at Bayern Munich. His second spell lasts from 1988 to 1995 and his final statistics read: 467 appearances, 163 goals. As a Red he won an impressive two Premier League titles, three FA Cups, one League Cup, three Charity Shields, the Cup Winners' Cup and UEFA Super Cup.

THE PLAYERS

United fans always reserve a special place in their affections for homegrown players, and Norman Whiteside is certainly one of those who made an instant impression on the Old Trafford faithful. He made his debut at the age of 16, stepping off the bench in United's Division One fixture at Brighton & Hove Albion in April 1982. That summer he'd play at the *Espana '82* World Cup for Northern Ireland, and then came his breakthrough campaign at club level. In 1982/83, he became the first United player to score in both domestic cup finals in the same season – ending the campaign with his first winners' medal (the FA Cup, 1983). Two years later he was the hero at Wembley again, this time hitting the extra-time winner against Everton to bring him a second FA Cup triumph (1985). Whiteside played a part in eight seasons for the Reds, although injury problems contributed to him leaving for Everton in July 1989.

OLD MANCHESTER UNITED IN COLOUR

Norman Whiteside wears a fan's flat cap as he leaves the pitch after FA Cup semi-final victory against Arsenal at Villa Park, on 16 April 1983. The Northern Irishman was the toast of the club after firing a stunning winner against the Gunners, as the Reds fight back from 1-0 down at half-time to win 2-1 and reach a second Wembley final of the season. The League Cup final had ended in defeat to Liverpool, but it was a different story (eventually) in the FA Cup final with Brighton & Hove Albion beaten 4-0 in a replay. Whiteside, already a man for the big occasion despite being only 18, scores United's second goal to become the (then) youngest scorer in a Cup final.

THE PLAYERS

BUSBY'S BABES

In the mid-1950s there emerged a team good enough to match anything in United's history, a side built on youth and vigour that captured the imagination of a nation – only to be tragically cut down in their prime…

OLD MANCHESTER UNITED IN COLOUR

Above: Matt Busby's bunch of bouncing Babes became the best side in England in the mid-1950s, and here are put through their paces in a training session in Blackpool in 1957.

Sixty-five years on, 6 February 1958 remains the central day in Manchester United history. When the Munich Air Disaster claimed the lives of eight first-team players and three members of Matt Busby's staff, and 23 people overall, it irrevocably changed the club's past, present and future.

The Busby Babes, as they are now known, were the greatest team in England, and perhaps the greatest club side that the country had ever seen, period. And though those few devastating seconds in Bavaria have immortalised those who lost their lives, the tragic ending to the story sometimes threatens to overshadow what Matt Busby's pioneering, thrilling young team actually achieved on the pitch during those brief but brilliant few years.

Manchester United had started to lay the seeds for its 1950s youth explosion in 1932, when the club created an 'A' team – a third side, below the first team and the reserves – which was primarily designed to developing young players from the local area. The Manchester United Junior Athletic Club (MUJAC) was formed in 1938 as a "schoolboy football scheme" that aspired to provide training facilities and coaching support for youngsters.

Matt Busby did not arrive at Old Trafford until after the Second World War, of course, but when he did begin his stint at the club, he benefitted hugely from the youth foundations that had been set by James W Gibson (chairman), Walter Crickmer (secretary) and Louis Rocca (scout) years beforehand. When Busby claimed his first major piece of silverware, the 1948 FA Cup, the winning XI included Jack Crompton, John Anderson, John Aston, Charlie Mitten and Johnny Morris – all players from the club's own youth stable.

But Busby's vision for youth – and that of his crucial assistant, Jimmy Murphy – was even bolder. The idea was to find players at a young age whose instincts matched and complemented those of the team-mates

around them; to harness a fluidity and a confidence that opponents would find impossible to stop. Undeniably, there was also a financial advantage to unearthing the country's best talents at a young age, thereby avoid expensive forays into the transfer market.

So Busby and Murphy set out around the United Kingdom, and hired an army of scouts to aid them in their recruitment drive. The result, after many careful hours of player development, was a gold rush of talent unlike any seen before or since. "We started a new wave from the bottom," explained Murphy, years later. "The game is all about experience and judgment and you can't buy judgment. And what a new wave it proved! All those kids who were later dubbed 'the Busby Babes' were reared there on the spot – fellows like Duncan Edwards, Bobby Charlton, Eddie Colman, David Pegg and others. It was wonderfully rewarding and exciting to see them develop into great players who brought fame to the club and to themselves. It was like watching little apples grow."

"It was wonderfully rewarding and exciting to see them develop into great players who brought fame to the club and to themselves. It was like watching little apples grow"

The introduction of the FA Youth Cup in 1952 shed a new spotlight on youth football, and United were in a perfect position to make hay. The club won the first five editions of the tournament, powered by the legendary Duncan Edwards and other star players like Eddie Colman, Billy Whelan, David Pegg and Bobby Charlton. Before long, these prodigies were let loose into the first team, as Busby responded to a difficult period of form by opting to empower the youngsters at his disposal.

The team that eventually became dubbed 'the Busby Babes' was not purely assembled

OLD MANCHESTER UNITED IN COLOUR

from home-reared youth talent – they were some key transfer acquisitions, such as Ray Wood (Darlington) and Tommy Taylor (Barnsley). But the soulful core of the team was indisputably homegrown, with Gorton-born captain Roger Byrne its most senior figure. Alongside him was a staggering smorgasbord of options. The aforementioned Edwards was arguably the pick of the Babes' squad list, but 'Big Duncan' was just the tip of the iceberg. The names reel off the tongue: Foulkes. Colman. Jones. Blanchflower. Whelan. Charlton. Viollet. Pegg. Scanlon. And there were many more behind them, champing at the bit to get a look-in.

Remarkably, once the young starlets formed the majority of the first team's starting XI, all the fluidity and confidence that Busby and Murphy had worked to instil came flooding out. They blitzed to the First Division title by 11 points in 1955/56. And by eight points the following season. In that 1956/57 campaign – the club's first in Europe – the Babes battered home an astonishing 143 goals at an average of 2.5 per game. No United team in the club's history has ever come close to matching that tally. The starting XI's average

The Munich Air Disaster meant that we would never find out just how far into the stratosphere the Babes might have soared

was just 22 years old. The Babes reached the European Cup semi-finals at the first attempt, only falling to a mighty Real Madrid side that would triumph for five consecutive seasons from the competition's inception.

Maybe Busby's marvellous young side could have hastened the end of Real's domination. Alas, the Munich Air Disaster of February 1958 meant that we would never find out just how far into the stratosphere the Babes might have soared. Munich was such a heartbreakingly unfair conclusion for a team that was all about effervescence and the expression of youth, but it happened, robbing millions of football fans of numerous generational talents. Byrne and Taylor

Below: The Babes' European Cup adventure took them all across the continent, and here they are pictured at Manchester Ringway Airport boarding a flight to Belgrade on 3 February 1958.

BUSBY'S BABES

Above: The wreckage of Flight BEA 609 lies in a snow-covered field close to Munich-Riem airport on 6 February 1958. Eight players and three members of staff were among the 23 people killed in the tragic accident.

were England mainstays. Colman, Pegg and Whelan were bewitching attacking talents who dazzled audiences everywhere they went. Mark Jones and Geoff Bent redoubtable defenders. And many who saw Duncan Edwards – just 21 at the time of his death – remain certain that he would have blossomed into one of the game's greatest-ever players. In defence, in midfield, and going forward, Edwards was already a totemic presence who could do everything elite competitive football required of a man. Even better, he was blessed with an easy-going, yet steely confidence that seemed impenetrable.

The disaster's toll went far beyond those that perished, too. Johnny Berry would never play again, nor Jackie Blanchflower. And who knows what mental demons those who survived had to deal with during the ensuing decades? Players like Bobby Charlton, Bill Foulkes and Harry Gregg were not fond of talking about themselves and their own troubles, given what their less fortunate mates had suffered, but their mere body language often hinted at the deep scarring left by the trauma they had experienced.

The Busby Babes set the club's eternal standards for youth, courage and success; a standard United is compelled to always try and match

From the club's perspective, the footballing excellence and youthful brio of the Babes spread the United gospel far and wide. The tragic denouement to their tale turned their story into immediate legend, and made the fortunes of Manchester United a matter of emotional importance to people all around the world. Not just in 1958, but forever. Because the Busby Babes set the club's eternal standards for youth, courage and success; a standard that the club is compelled to always try and match. Even now, all these decades on, their stunning, sad story inspires both joy and melancholy in equal measure.

OLD MANCHESTER UNITED IN COLOUR

BUSBY'S BABES

United manager Matt Busby shares some words of wisdom with members of his first-team squad ahead of a training session in Blackpool in March 1957. Pictured are (left to right): Dennis Viollet, Tommy Taylor, David Pegg, trainer Tom Curry, Wilf McGuinness, club captain Roger Byrne, manager Matt Busby, goalkeeper Ray Wood, Liam Whelan, Duncan Edwards, Mark Jones, Geoff Bent and Johnny Berry. Busby would often take his side for short breaks to Blackpool's Norbreck Hydro hotel to escape the glare of attention, a change of scenery, and to enhance team bonding. His side were already champions of England when this photograph was taken (winning the First Division championship in 1956) and were well on course to retain their title and reach the 1957 FA Cup final – sadly, losing 1-2 to Aston Villa at Wembley to miss out on the league and Cup 'Double'.

OLD MANCHESTER UNITED IN COLOUR

Here come the Babes! Roger Byrne leads the United players on to the Old Trafford pitch ahead of the 63rd Manchester derby, on 31 December 1955. To the right of Byrne is outside-right Johnny Berry, with outside-left John Doherty and full-back Bill Foulkes following behind. A crowd of 60,956 watched the Reds defeat Manchester City 2-1 – with second-half goals from Tommy Taylor and Dennis Viollet overturning City's first-half strike from Jack Dyson. The victory kept United top of the First Division and showed how far the young Reds had come in a short space of time; Busby's side having been beaten 5-0 at home by Les McDowall's Blues the previous season, and 1-0 at Maine Road just three months earlier. Skipper Byrne was a natural leader, one of the senior members of the squad despite being aged only 26, and was skipper from 1955 until his death in the Munich Air Disaster in February 1958.

BUSBY'S BABES

Left: United's youth team pose for a photo outside their hotel in Bangor, Northern Ireland, during the 1953/54 season. Pictured are (back row, l-r): Ian Greaves, Walter Whitehurst, Tommy Barratt, Gordon Clayton, Alan Rhodes, Paddy Kennedy, Brace Fulton, hotel manager (name unknown); (middle row, l-r) Eddie Lewis, trainer Bill Inglis, chief coach Jimmy Murphy, coach Bert Whalley, Noel McFarlane; (front row, l-r) Sammy Chapman, Eddie Colman, Duncan Edwards, Billy Whelan and Albert Scanlon.

Right: United were holders of the FA Youth Cup from its inception in 1953 until 1957 – with this side achieving the third of those five Cup wins. Pictured are: (back row, l-r) Duncan Edwards, Terry Beckett, Shay Brennan, Tony Hawksworth, Alan Rhodes, John Queenan; (front row) Peter Jones, Dennis Fidler, Eddie Colman, Wilf McGuinness and Bobby Charlton.

OLD MANCHESTER UNITED IN COLOUR

25 April 1957: United captain Roger Byrne shakes hands with Real Madrid skipper Miguel Munoz (left) ahead of kick-off in a European Cup semi-final second-leg match at Old Trafford. It was the culmination of a thrilling first season in competitive continental competition for the Babes, having overcome Anderlecht, Borussia Dortmund and Athletic Club en route to the final four. Old Trafford's first European game played under floodlights ended as a 2-2 draw, with Real progressing 5-3 on aggregate and going on to retain the European Cup. Although disappointed, Busby's boys had shown enough promise against Europe's benchmark side to encourage many an expert to believe that the Reds would soon be challenging for *Los Blancos'* European crown.

Such was the popularity of the Babes, pictured here ahead of a home league fixture in December 1957, that a song was written in their honour. The *Manchester United Calypso* was released by Edric Connor in 1957, and remains a song still sung by fans at matches to this day. It reflected the excitement surrounding the Babes – a nickname first given to Busby's young side by the UK press in January 1953 – and includes the famous line: "If ever they're playing in your town, get yourself to that football ground." In this particular starting line-up are: (back, l-r) Duncan Edwards, Bill Foulkes, Mark Jones, Ray Wood, Eddie Colman, David Pegg; (front, l-r): Johnny Berry, Liam Whelan, Roger Byrne, Tommy Taylor and Dennis Viollet. Tragically, seven of these players would perish in Munich less than two months later.

OLD MANCHESTER UNITED IN COLOUR

Such was the strength in depth of the United youth system, overseen by the indomitable Jimmy Murphy, that Busby enjoyed the luxury of being able to rotate his squad decades before it became *de rigueur*. If injury struck down one first-team regular, another would step up from the all-conquering Reserves. The Reds' impressive scouting system meant players were discovered way beyond the boundaries of Manchester and Salford – as the team photo above demonstrates (left to right): Ray Wood (from County Durham), Duncan Edwards (Dudley, West Midlands), Tommy Taylor (Yorkshire), Liam Whelan (Dublin, Ireland), Geoff Bent (Salford), Bill Foulkes (St Helens), Jackie Blanchflower (Belfast, Northern Ireland), Colin Webster (Cardiff, Wales), Dennis Viollet (Manchester), Eddie Colman (Salford) and Johnny Berry (Aldershot). All led by Scotsman Matt Busby and Welshman Jimmy Murphy.

BUSBY'S BABES

United faced opposition from the Football League in entering the European Cup in 1956/57, but Busby recognised continental football as the next step for club football and refused to be swayed, taking the Babes on a new exciting adventure. As shown below, the United players looked like film stars but were more like excited kids when departing for various new football destinations. Here they are pictured at Manchester Airport making their way towards their plane ahead of a flight to Madrid to face the mighty Real, on 9 April 1957. Pictured are (left to right): Bill Foulkes, Ray Wood, Billy Whelan, Johnny Berry, Gordon Clayton, Dennis Viollet, Colin Webster, Duncan Edwards, Tommy Taylor, David Pegg and Bobby Charlton. Destinations visited by the Babes prior to the air crash were Brussels, Dortmund, Bilbao, Madrid, Dublin, Prague and Belgrade.

OLD MANCHESTER UNITED IN COLOUR

BUSBY'S BABES

The last line-up: United's players stand shoulder-to-shoulder ahead of the Reds' European Cup quarter-final second-leg at Red Star Belgrade on 5 February 1958. Five of these players, plus three other squad members, would lose their lives on a Munich runway the following day, making this an image known by United supporters the world over. The eleven selected by Matt Busby are (left to right): Duncan Edwards, Eddie Colman, Mark Jones, Kenny Morgans, Bobby Charlton, Dennis Viollet, Tommy Taylor, Bill Foulkes, Harry Gregg, Albert Scanlon and Roger Byrne. Goals from Viollet and Charlton (2) gave United a seemingly unassailable 3-0 half-time lead (5-1 on aggregate) only for the Yugoslavian side to fight back to 3-3 in the second half. Thankfully the Babes held on for a 5-4 aggregate win, although a tragic twist of fate would deny many in this side the chance to fulfill their dream of European Cup glory.

OLD MANCHESTER UNITED IN COLOUR

Manchester mourns as coffins for some of the victims of the Munich Air Disaster are repatriated from Germany on 8 February 1958. Tens of thousands lined the 12-mile route from the airport to Old Trafford, with a police car and motorbike escorting 10 hearses to the stadium – where they were placed overnight in the gymnasium on tables draped in black cloth. Those along the route stood in solemn silence, some quietly weeping, others saying prayers, as the Manchester public, regardless of whether they were Red or Blue, united in mourning of all those lost. The eventual death toll reached 23: eight players, three club staff, eight journalists, plus four passengers and crew. They shall never be forgotten.

OLD MANCHESTER UNITED IN COLOUR

It wasn't just Manchester that mourned the tragedy of Munich. Respects were paid all across the football world, including (below) in Amsterdam the weekend after the accident. Black armbands and a minute's silences took place wherever matches were played, although United's own immediate fixtures were understandably postponed. With manager Matt Busby fighting for his life in Munich's Rechts der Isar hospital, Jimmy Murphy and club chairman Harold Hardman, plus the club's small group of staff, set about ensuring the club could continue. However, following the funerals and remembrance services, attention quickly turned to finding a way to field a team to play United's FA Cup fifth-round tie against Sheffield Wednesday at Old Trafford. Youngsters stepped up, signings arrived, joining crash survivors fit enough to play.

BUSBY'S BABES

Crash survivor Bill Foulkes leads out the United team for the first match after the Munich Air Disaster, on 19 February 1958. The matchday programme carries a defiant message on the front cover – 'United will go on!' – but also includes a Reds line-up on the inside pages with blank spaces left for the names of the players, such is the uncertainty about who will represent the team this night. Thousands of fans are locked outside as 59,848 cram into Old Trafford to not only pay their respects to the lost Babes, but to cheer the Reds to an unlikely FA Cup win against fellow First Division side Sheffield Wednesday. Joining Foulkes in the starting XI is fellow crash survivor Harry Gregg, pictured in the green shirt (above), a man dubbed the 'Hero of Munich' after he returned to the broken plane to pull four passengers clear of the wreckage: a mother and her 22-month old baby, plus team-mates Bobby Charlton and Dennis Viollet.

New United skipper Bill Foulkes shakes hands with Sheffield Wednesday captain Albert Quixall, who would later move to the Reds, ahead of United's first post-Munich fixture. Stand-in manager Jimmy Murphy gives debuts to four new players, with Shay Brennan and Alex Dawson stepping up from the youth ranks to join emergency new signings Stan Crowther (signed from Aston Villa) and Ernie Taylor (from Blackpool). On an emotion-filled night, the crowd roar the Reds to a 3-0 victory courtesy of a brace from Brennan (one directly from a corner) and a goal from Dawson. For Foulkes, it was a bittersweet evening under the Old Trafford floodlights as he replaced the deceased Roger Byrne as United captain. "When I was a lad, I used to dream that one day I would captain a great team like United," the big defender later reflected. "Now my dream has come true – but I wish it hadn't."

OLD MANCHESTER UNITED IN COLOUR

'Murphy's Marvels' kept their unlikely FA Cup run going all the way to Wembley, where they took on Bolton Wanderers in the final on 3 May 1958. Following the win against Sheffield Wednesday, the Reds saw off West Brom in a replay in the quarter-final, then Fulham in another replay in the semi-final. Two more survivors of the crash had resumed playing by the time of the final – Bobby Charlton and Dennis Viollet – and Matt Busby, walking with a stick, was well enough to attend the showpiece game. It was something of a fairytale that United should even have reached the final given the circumstances, but that was where the storybook ending stopped as Bolton came out 2-0 victors thanks to a brace from Nat Lofthouse. Still, United had begun the rebuilding process and shown that the days of glory were not over.

THE MANAGERS

From Ernest Mangnall to Alex Ferguson, the black-and-white photographic era saw many different characters take charge of the United first-team (with varying degrees of success!). Here are some of the Reds' bosses from down the decades…

OLD MANCHESTER UNITED IN COLOUR

Above: Matt Busby is regarded as the man who shaped the modern club, and here he shakes hands with the Duke of Edinburgh ahead of a charity match in aid of the Variety Club against Manchester City at Maine Road, in May 1964.

The achievements of managers Matt Busby and Alex Ferguson at Manchester United were resounding enough to earn both a knighthood and an indelible place in football folklore, but while they may be the legends of club history, they are far from the only noteworthy figures to take the Reds' managerial helm.

The post-Ferguson era of David Moyes, Louis van Gaal, Jose Mourinho, Ole Gunnar Solskjaer and Erik ten Hag – with cameos from interim managers Ryan Giggs, Michael Carrick and Ralf Rangnick – has played out in full glare of the world's media, but their early predecessors worked in a lower-key landscape which largely operated well away from the spotlight.

As Newton Heath's very first full-time employee, Alfred H Albut was essentially the club's first manager, taking charge of team affairs, administrative work and all points in-between from 1892 until 1900, when the role was adopted by James West. He, like Albut, had the unenviable task of keeping the Heathens' perilous financial situation in-hand, which he managed to do before the new regime under the ownership of John Henry Davies prompted the club's reinvention as Manchester United.

With Davies determined to take his Second Division club up to the top tier, he installed Ernest Mangnall, who had already built himself a reputation within the game as an astute footballing man who had experience as a director at Bolton Wanderers and a manager at Burnley. A combination of wise recruitment – which included key signings Charlie Roberts, Charlie Sagar and George Wall – and tactical acumen soon had the Reds on the up, and before long United were a First Division team. Mangnall's inspired transfer record continued ahead of the 1907/08 campaign with the show-stopping signing of Manchester City quartet Billy Meredith, Sandy Turnbull, Jimmy Bannister and Herbert Burgess, a bold move which played a major part in United's first-ever title triumph that term.

The first manager to bring major silverware to the club, Mangnall soon followed it up with the following term's FA Cup and then regained the championship in 1910/11, by which point he had helped the club's migration from North

THE MANAGERS

Above: Matt Busby shares words of wisdom with Reds youngsters (left to right) Duncan Edwards, Jackie Blanchflower and David Pegg at Old Trafford in January 1954.

In 1912/13, Mangnall moved to the Reds' cross-city rivals to become the first person to manage United and City, but that did nothing to besmirch his crucial work in establishing the Reds as a pre-War footballing force

Road to the new, gleaming Old Trafford. In a shock move early in the 1912/13 campaign, Mangnall moved to the Reds' cross-city rivals to become the first person to manage both United and City, but that did nothing to besmirch his crucial work in establishing the Reds as a pre-War footballing force.

Replacing Mangnall was no easy feat, with TJ Wallworth stepping in briefly as acting secretary and manager before JJ Bentley took the reins for just over two years until Boxing Day 1914. Jack Robson enjoyed an eventful six-year tenure which encompassed a dramatic relegation escape and the outbreak of the First World War, before he resigned through ill health in October 1921.

Relegation followed in the immediate aftermath of Robson's departure, with his replacement John Chapman unable to keep the Reds afloat. United's fortunes undulated during his five years at the helm before a sudden, mid-season departure for unspecified misconduct reasons prompted the groundbreaking installation of Clarence Hilditch as the Reds' first player-manager. The half-back fared well enough in the role to stave off relegation concerns, but he was restored to full-time playing staff with the appointment of Herbert Bamlett.

A former referee who had excelled expectations at the Oldham Athletic helm, taking the Latics to second in the First Division, Bamlett was installed at a time when United were a First Division club but struggling financially, and the Reds ultimately succumbed to relegation in his fourth and final campaign.

OLD MANCHESTER UNITED IN COLOUR

His subsequent dismissal prompted the promotion of club secretary Walter Crickmer, whose near-four decades of service to the club included two stints as manager. The first came at a time when new ownership was being sought, and Crickmer staved off relegation while James W Gibson purchased the club. The new owner duly allowed Walter to return to the secretarial position while Scott Duncan took charge of team matters and, alongside Gibson, Crickmer became a key component in the creation of United's youth development system. Duncan's sudden resignation in 1937 threw up another interim stint as manager for Crickmer before, with United back in the First Division, the outbreak of the Second World War put the competitive game on a hiatus.

By the time football resumed post-war in 1945, United had made an appointment which would reverberate through English football.

Former Manchester City and Liverpool right-half Matt Busby was approached by United's chief scout Louis Rocca and tempted into taking his first role in management at just 35.

"Call it confidence, conceit, arrogance or ignorance, but I was unequivocal about it," the Scot later admitted. "I would accept the managership of Manchester United only if they would let me have it all my own way. As the manager I would want to manage. I would be the boss."

As understatements go, Busby's proved emphatic. Despite taking on a club with an expectant fanbase, a bomb-damaged stadium and restricted finances, he quickly set about educating his players and coaxing the best from them. In his third season, United won the FA Cup. Four years later, the First Division followed, after which Busby set about introducing the fruits of the youth

"I would accept the managership of Manchester United only if they let me have it all my own way. As the manager I would want to manage. I would be the boss" - Sir Matt Busby

THE MANAGERS

Above: Coach Malcolm Musgrove (in the centre with his back to camera) and new United manager Frank O'Farrell (stood to his left) address the United players at The Cliff training ground ahead of pre-season training in July 1972.

system enacted by Crickmer and Gibson. His thrilling young side became known as the Busby Babes and won back-to-back titles in 1955/56 and 1956/57, also becoming English football's first entrants into the European Cup in the latter campaign.

The following term, determined to improve on a semi-final exit in 1957, United once again reached the last four but were decimated by the Munich Air Disaster. While Busby recuperated, assistant manager Jimmy Murphy temporarily took the helm, kept the Red flag flying high and steered the club through its darkest hour.

When Busby regained his health, he set about rebuilding the club again and, incredibly, needed only five years to bring silverware back to Old Trafford, winning the 1963 FA Cup. Two league titles quickly followed before the ultimate achievement: winning the European Cup for the first time in 1968. His work complete, Busby stepped down in 1969 and, though he briefly replaced successor Wilf McGuinness the following season, the Scot retired for good in June 1971.

Thereafter, the expectations around United made life hard for those who followed. Frank O'Farrell lasted 18 months, Tommy Docherty helmed relegation but then bounced back with immediate promotion and success in the 1977 FA Cup, while Dave Sexton struggled to coax consistency from his side before the arrival of Ron Atkinson in 1981. The charismatic Atkinson won the FA Cup in both 1983 and 1985, but his inability to sustain a title tilt prompted his departure in 1986, at which point United's board looked north for a solution once again.

Plucked from Aberdeen, where his demolition of the Old Firm duopoly had laid bare his abilities, Alex Ferguson strode into Old Trafford determined to have a deep and lasting impact. Writing in the first *United Review* after Ferguson's appointment, legendary Manchester football scribe David Meek foretold: "I warned him that with a club the size of Manchester United, trying to meet all the demands of the public will be like trying to fill a bucket with a hole in it. But I don't think it is going to stop him trying, because behind this rather idealistic philosophy lies a manager of great determination. Sir Matt Busby started at Old Trafford with this outlook on life... and he didn't do too badly!"

The rest, of course, is history.

OLD MANCHESTER UNITED IN COLOUR

Pictured is club secretary Walter Crickmer (left) with manager Scott Duncan, on 1 November 1935. Duncan was in charge of the Reds' first team from July 1932 until November 1937, overseeing what have widely come to be known as United's 'yo-yo years'. Having taken over with the Old Trafford club in the Second Division, it took four seasons for Duncan's Reds to win promotion back to English football's top tier – finally achieving it in 1935/36. However, the joy was short-lived as his side were promptly relegated in 1936/37, and still struggling at the time of his resignation (six defeats from the first 14 games of 1937/38). Scott moved on to Ipswich Town and was replaced by the ever-reliable club stalwart Crickmer, who duly helped United win instant promotion back to the top flight.

OLD MANCHESTER UNITED IN COLOUR

THE MANAGERS

Little did they know at the time, but within this photograph is the future of Manchester football. Taken in 1939, the image shows international players Joe Mercer of Everton and England (left), Matt Busby of Liverpool and Scotland (centre), and Don Welsh of Charlton Athletic and England. The trio were part of the Army Physical Training Corps, based at barracks in Aldershot but also serving behind allied lines in France, Italy and Greece. At the end of the Second World War, Busby would become United manager after the club's 'fixer' Louis Rocca approached him to replace secretary Walter Crickmer as first-team boss. Don Welsh hung up his boots in 1947 and was later Liverpool manager from 1951-56. Mercer was younger, however, and would continue playing after the war, representing Arsenal until 1954. Following successful spells as manager at Sheffield United and Aston Villa, Mercer became Manchester City boss in 1965, where he would win five trophies before departing Maine Road in 1971.

OLD MANCHESTER UNITED IN COLOUR

The Manchester United that Busby took over was in a sorry state off the pitch, with Old Trafford unusable and the club groundsharing Maine Road with his old club Manchester City. In far better condition was the team he inherited and built upon, and he quickly turned the Reds into a formidable outfit that finished second in the First Division in four of his first five seasons, and won the FA Cup in 1948. The title was finally United's in 1951/52, after a 41-year absence, by which point the club were back playing at Old Trafford and with a youth system that was flourishing. Pictured is Busby sat at his desk in 1957, with his young side once again the toast of English football.

THE MANAGERS

One aspect of strong management is to surround yourself with the right people, and Busby wasted little time in bringing in Jimmy Murphy as his chief coach (and later assistant manager). The pair had met during the Second World War in Bari, Italy, in 1945, when Murphy was giving a lecture on football tactics to a group of soldiers. Busby asked him to become his assistant at United, and so began one of the great management pairings. Also on Busby's coaching staff was the hugely admired Bert Whalley, who is pictured here with Murphy at Old Trafford on 11 October 1955. Tragically, Whalley was one of 23 people killed in the Munich Air Disaster in 1958.

Matt Busby poses for a portrait during the 1947/48 season, looking every inch the godfather of Manchester United that he would become. The Scotsman, born in Bellshill, Lanarkshire, would take the Reds not only to the top of the English game with three different sides but also to international fame by winning the European Cup in 1968. His philosophy was simple but striking, always telling his team to go out and enjoy themselves. Between 1945 and 1971 his teams did just that, thrilling huge crowds wherever they played and winning five Football League titles, two FA Cups, five Charity Shields (two of which were shared) and the European Cup. At the time of this photograph he was about to win the first of those trophies, the FA Cup at Wembley in 1948, and he later said of his approach to his role as manager: "I never wanted Manchester United to be second to anybody. Only the best would be good enough."

THE MANAGERS

Supporting Matt Busby in his quest to make United the best was Jimmy Murphy, whose eye for a player, masterly coaching and passionate speeches so impressed the Reds boss. He worked for the club for 43 years, but never with more fervour than in the aftermath of the Munich Air Disaster in February 1958, when he stepped in as caretaker manager with Busby fighting for his life in a Bavarian hospital. The Welshman had missed the trip due his other role as Wales manager, leading them to the 1958 World Cup finals with a victory against Israel. Upon his return to Old Trafford he was informed of the accident and left the grim task of notifying the families of the deceased, visiting the injured in Munich, attending the many funerals, and then somehow putting a team together to compete for United in three competitions. While the league form suffered for all the many changes, and the European Cup semi-final proved a step too far for the new charges, Murphy somehow led his hurriedly assembled side to the FA Cup final. a 0-2 defeat to Bolton Wanderers was not the fairytale ending many were hoping for, but he'd helped ensure through his devotion that Manchester United Football Club would continue and rise again.

OLD MANCHESTER UNITED IN COLOUR

THE MANAGERS

This image of Jimmy Murphy and Matt Busby sat in a dugout is from August 1967, at the start of an unforgettable season for Manchester United. In the 54th game of a campaign in which the Reds had been pipped to the Football League title on the final day by Manchester City, Busby's side defeated Benfica 4-1 after extra-time to become the first English winners of the European Cup. For these two men it was the realisation of a long held shared dream to see United as the kings of the continent.

THE MANAGERS

28 May 1968: Busby surveys the Wembley pitch as his players carry out last preparations on the eve of European football's elite club final. Behind him is United physio Ted Dalton, who plays a vital role the next night in helping ease aching muscles when the final against the Portuguese champions goes into extra-time. Busby, who enjoys a kickabout during the Wembley training session, leads his side to a thrilling 4-1 victory against the Lisbon club, with Bobby Charlton (2), George Best and Brian Kidd scoring the decisive goals. United's line-up contains seven homegrown players, including Charlton and Bill Foulkes who survived the Munich Air Disaster just over a decade earlier.

OLD MANCHESTER UNITED IN COLOUR

14 January 1969: A throng of press and photographers pack into an Old Trafford lounge for the announcement that Sir Matt Busby is to step down as United manager at the end of the 1968/69 season. He announces to the room: "It's time to make way for a younger man, a tracksuited manager. United is no longer just a football club. It is an institution. I feel the demands are beyond one human being." Five months later, Wilf McGuinness steps up from his role as Reserves manager to take over first-team affairs, with Busby moving 'upstairs' to become general manager. Aged 59, and approaching a quarter of a century at the helm, Sir Matt insists it is the right time to leave the role – stressing it is nothing to do with the three successive defeats that had preceded the announcement. "It has been a wonderful life," adds Busby. "It has been a demanding one but wonderful."

THE MANAGERS

OLD MANCHESTER UNITED IN COLOUR

Here's Sir Matt again, pictured ten years after the crowning glory of his career at Wembley stadium – that balmy, emotion-filled night when Benfica were beaten and the over-sized trophy thrown into the London air. He is now a club director at Old Trafford and here he's busy sorting through post in what is United's Centenary year – which is marked by a celebration match against Real Madrid (which, for the record, Dave Sexton's side won 4-0). Two years later Busby is appointed club president.

THE MANAGERS

Matt Busby was the winner of many awards for his services to football, culminating in his knighthood in July 1968. Among other earlier awards is this one, presented to him in December 1964: the newly-created Football Sword of Honour, given to him at a presentation in Manchester. The Scot is the first recipient of the sword for 'distinguished service to British and international football' and is pictured here with several familiar faces. Second from the left is his former United player Dennis Viollet, Harry Gregg is stood behind Busby, while second from the right is his good friend (and Liverpool manager) Bill Shankly, with Maurice Setters on the far right of the photo.

OLD MANCHESTER UNITED IN COLOUR

Having stepped down from his role as first-team manager at the end of the 1968/69 season, Busby returned to take temporary charge for the last 21 games of 1970/71. Poor results had led to Wilf McGuinness being replaced and Busby returned to his former role until a new manager could be found. This photograph, taken on 9 January 1971, shows Sir Matt in the main stand at Stamford Bridge sat alongside Reds chairman Louis Edwards. A Willie Morgan penalty and late winner from Alan Gowling allow United to come from behind for a 2-1 victory against Chelsea in front of 53,482. Busby would step down again at the end of the season, with Leicester City's Frank O'Farrell a close season appointment. In his second spell, Sir Matt recorded 11 victories, with three draws and seven defeats.

THE MANAGERS

OLD MANCHESTER UNITED IN COLOUR

28 September 1972: United manager Frank O'Farrell (left) is pictured with new signing Ted MacDougall (bought from Bournemouth for £195,000). O'Farrell was United manager from 1 July 1971 to 19 December 1972, replacing Sir Matt Busby, who had returned to the Reds dugout after the sacking of Wilf McGuinness (who was in charge of the first-team from June 1969-December 1970). The post-Busby era was a turbulent time for the Reds, to say the least, and this picture is testament to that. Less than three months after this image was taken, Irishman O'Farrell was relieved of his duties and new boss Tommy Docherty swiftly moved MacDougall on, selling him to West Ham United after just 18 games and five goals in March 1973. O'Farrell's managerial record at United? He oversaw 81 matches and recorded 30 wins, with 24 draws and 27 defeats.

THE MANAGERS

OLD MANCHESTER UNITED IN COLOUR

THE MANAGERS

Tommy's Docherty's time as United manager came to a controversial end, but Reds fans of a certain vintage will always look back fondly at his time in charge. Indeed, many believe Docherty was on course to bring the Football League title back to Old Trafford at the time of his dismissal in July 1977. 'Doc' replaced Frank O'Farrell as Old Trafford boss in December 1972, and although his side suffered the shock of relegation in 1973/74, the thrilling playing style of his team brought promotion the following season, a genuine title challenge in 1975/76, plus two FA Cup final appearances in 1976 and '77 (defeat to Southampton in the former, victory against Liverpool in the latter). In this photo, Docherty and his then assistant Paddy Crerand are in the visitors' dugout at Stamford Bridge on 30 March 1974. The Reds won the game 3-1 amidst a late-season surge that sadly proved too late to save United from the drop into the Second Division. Crerand left United in 1976, later becoming Northampton Town manager, and Docherty was sacked in a blaze of publicity a year later following off-field revelations in the aftermath of that FA Cup final triumph.

12 August 1978: United manager Dave Sexton signs autographs for supporters during an open day at Old Trafford, where fans have come to watch a public first-team training session. Sexton was Reds manager from July 1977 to April 1981, but silverware proved elusive for him despite reaching the 1979 FA Cup final (losing 2-3 to Arsenal) and a second-placed finished in First Division in 1979/80. Fans were not great admirers of his team's often pragmatic style of play and so support for him slowly dwindled in his final season in charge – the Reds eventually finishing eighth in 1980/81.

THE MANAGERS

OLD MANCHESTER UNITED IN COLOUR

Ron Atkinson holds up a bottle of champagne in one hand while brandishing a cigar in the other, on 10 August 1981. The ebullient Liverpudlian was just two months into his role as United manager, having arrived from West Bromwich Albion. The ever-positive Atkinson was clearly looking forward to the challenge ahead, and although his tenure would begin with two defeats and two draws from his first four matches, good times were coming. In his first season, 1981/82, the Reds signed England international Bryan Robson from his old club West Brom for a British record fee of £1.5million. 'Big Ron' described his new signing as "pure gold", a label countlessly justified over the next 13 years. In that first season, Atkinson's United led Division One for long periods only for Liverpool (who else!) to eventually take the title. Still, the style of play had captured the imagination of the fans and silverware was just a season away.

THE MANAGERS

OLD MANCHESTER UNITED IN COLOUR

THE MANAGERS

Just over two months after the previous photograph, Atkinson is feeling very much at home in his new office at The Cliff training ground. Two days earlier his side had travelled to Anfield and pulled off a stunning 2-1 win against Liverpool, thanks to an 89th-minute strike from Arthur Albiston. Big Ron would enjoy plenty of other memorable moments as Reds' manager, including two FA Cup triumphs in 1983 and 1985, but it was the league championship that everyone connected to the club craved most. And after falling short in 1985/86, having topped the table for much of the season, the writing was on the wall for Atkinson. After winning just five of the first 17 games of 1986/87, his reign came to an end.

OLD MANCHESTER UNITED IN COLOUR

Manchester United's new manager Alex Ferguson makes his way towards the players' entrance at Oxford United's Manor Ground stadium, ahead of the first of his 1,500 matches as Reds' boss. Two days after his switch from Aberdeen, on 6 November 1986, where he'd enjoyed huge success in breaking the grip that Celtic and Rangers had long held over the Scottish game, he took charge of the Reds' First Division fixture at Oxford. It was to be an inauspicious start, with a 13,545 crowd watching the hosts clinch a 2-0 victory over the Reds – however, despite this slow-burner of a start, a new and (eventually) glorious era had begun.

OLD MANCHESTER UNITED IN COLOUR

Alex Ferguson once described his greatest challenge as United manager being to knock Liverpool off their perch, and here he is pictured in the thick of it at Anfield on 4 April 1988. It would be another five years before United would be champions of England, ending an agonising 26-year wait, but in this Easter fixture from 1987/88 some of the traits that would become ingrained in Ferguson's sides were very much on show. With an hour gone, United were 1-3 down and reduced to 10 men after the sending off of Colin Gibson. Anfield is raucous, scenting blood, but Ferguson remains calm. He brings on Norman Whiteside to add some steel in midfield and it changes the course of the game. Attacking the Kop end, Bryan Robson reduces the deficit with a deflected shot, then Gordon Strachan scurries clear of the Liverpool defence to slot home an equaliser with 13 minutes left – celebrating by smoking an imaginary cigar. Bigger challenges were to come in the next few years, but an important marker for the future had been laid down.

THE MANAGERS

GLORY, GLORY

United have had countless memorable matches, many inspirational managers, and some truly iconic players, but what lives longest in the memory is always success – as shown in these trophy-winning images...

OLD MANCHESTER UNITED IN COLOUR

Above: United players and officials at the Midland Hotel in Manchester for a celebration dinner after winning the the 1935/1936 Second Division championship.

Success, on its own, does not completely explain the incredible worldwide affection that exists for Manchester United. Certain romantic notions undoubtedly underpin much of the adoration; notions which are often tied to factors like the Busby Babes, the Munich Air Disaster or the 'United Trinity' of Best, Law and Charlton. You probably hold your own personal opinion. But who really knows what goes into that unique and magical cocktail mix?

What is undeniable is that United are among the most successful clubs in world football when it comes to trophies. And while silverware might not be the only ingredient behind our popularity, it's a fairly crucial one. Domestically, United have more top-flight titles than any other English club (20). Add the country's two other major trophies into the equation (the FA Cup and the League Cup) and, overall, United have 38 pieces of silverware compared to Liverpool's 36. Both are far ahead of the country's next-most successful outfits.

The Merseysiders might lead the way when it comes to European Cups (now known as the Champions League), with six successes to our three, but Europe is no less significant in United's history. Far from it. The Reds were the very first English club to take part in European football and, but for the tragedy at Munich, might well have claimed the famous trophy much earlier than 1968.

The club's earliest landmark statements were delivered under the watch of manager Ernest Mangnall, who led United to a maiden First Division title in 1907/08 and an inaugural FA Cup triumph the following season, when the Reds overcame Bristol City at Crystal Palace thanks to a solitary goal from Sandy

Busby's radical reimagining of United was only just beginning. After that 1951/52 title, he integrated reams of talent that the club's youth programme had quietly been nurturing behind the scenes

Turnbull. A second championship arrived in 1910/11, before Mangnall left to take charge of local rivals Manchester City in 1912.

Remarkably, United would not scale such peaks again until the first of two legendary managers, Matt Busby, rocked up at a war-ravaged Old Trafford in 1945. The Scotsman reached his true zenith in the 1950s and 1960s, but he quickly made a seismic impact at the club, memorably leading the Reds to a thrilling 4-2 victory over Blackpool in the 1948 FA Cup final. After four second-placed league finishes in five years, he then added the First Division in 1951/52, ending the club's 41-year wait for a third domestic top-flight championship.

But Busby's radical reimagining of United was only just beginning. In the years after that 1951/52 title, he successfully integrated reams of talent that the club's youth programme had quietly been nurturing behind the scenes. In 1956, the team that history would immortalise as the 'Busby Babes' swept to domestic glory via a whopping margin of 11 points (when just

OLD MANCHESTER UNITED IN COLOUR

Above: United and Liverpool players put rivalries aside to wave to the Wembley crowd after drawing 0-0 in the 1977 Charity Shield, sharing the trophy in the process.

two were awarded for a win). It was arguably the most dominant First Division campaign of the 20th century up to that point. The following season, they near enough repeated it, finishing eight points clear of Tottenham Hotspur and Preston North End.

During this spell, Busby also led Manchester United into Europe – against the myopic advice of the Football League – kickstarting the English game's long and dramatic association with continental football. The Babes reached the semi-finals at the first time of asking, only to fall to a godlike Real Madrid team. But the direction of the United side was clear: here was a squad brimming with youthful zest, with a zeal for expression and attacking football, poised to transfer its domestic supremacy onto a fresh European canvas.

Sadly, Munich denied the Babes a shot at a third consecutive league triumph and becoming the first British team to lift the European Cup – and left United fans with a forever unanswerable 'What if?' hanging over the potential of arguably our greatest-ever team. That the club has still won more league titles than any other English team, and managed three European Cups, is a

That the club has won more league titles than any other English team, and managed three European Cups, is a cause for immense pride

cause for immense pride, if you consider what could have happened to United post-Munich. One only needs to look at Torino FC, who were champions of *Serie A* for five consecutive seasons in the 1940s, before the Superga air disaster of 1949 robbed them of almost their entire team. In the years since, the *Granata* have been crowned champions of Italy just once.

For Busby and United, Munich forced an unavoidable period of harrowing reflection and reconsolidation. The Reds were almost relegated in 1963 but, spurred on by new arrivals Paddy Crerand and Denis Law, managed to lift the FA Cup at the end of that season by beating Leicester City 3-1. Like the

1948 success – Busby's first major trophy – the cup triumph of '63 proposed the shape of the better things to come. Bolstered by new stars from the junior ranks – David Sadler, Nobby Stiles and future *Ballon d'Or* winner George Best among them – United went on to seize the English title in 1965 and 1967, before finally fulfilling Busby's greatest dream a year later.

As noted earlier, Liverpool might currently boast more European Cups, but United's intimate relationship with the competition remains baked into football myth. When the side Busby built from the ashes of Munich finally conquered the continent 10 years on, with a famous 4-1 victory over Benfica at Wembley, United became the first English name to be engraved on the trophy. But the achievement meant something more than even that. The club's resurrection, from a place of darkness that few football teams have ever experienced, established United as one of sport's greatest stories.

Busby departed as manager the following year, his ultimate quest finally complete, and the club entered a long wilderness period as it searched for a worthy managerial successor. Inexplicably, relegation followed just five years after the Scot stepped down, but success continued to flicker at Old Trafford.

The Second Division title is not considered a major trophy, but the manner in which Tommy Docherty led the post-relegation revival has become the stuff of legend. Roaring back into the First Division in 1975, the Doc's rampant United then reached the FA Cup final, only to lose to Southampton, and finished just four points adrift of eventual Division One champions Liverpool. But then, in '77, he orchestrated a memorable 2-1 FA Cup final win over the treble-chasing Merseysiders. Once again, in the hour of deepest need, the FA Cup had provided a taste of salvation. It would do so again, in both 1983 and 1985, under Ron Atkinson, as the search for Busby's true heir intensified amid sporadic ups and frustrating downs.

In 1986, the right man was finally found. Alex Ferguson would have to wait until the 1990s to complete the club's return to its rightful place at the top of the English and European game, but United's rich history offered him a clear and glorious template to follow.

Below: Welcome home! The European Cup is paraded on the streets of an English city for the first time, as United show off the trophy won so gloriously at Wembley the previous night.

GLORY, GLORY

All hail the conquering heroes! Huge crowds greet the Manchester United team the day after the Reds have beaten Bristol City 1-0 at the Crystal Palace in the FA Cup final, played on 24 April 1909. Charlie Roberts sits at the front of a horse-drawn carriage holding the Cup, with team-mate George Wall on his right and the other players sat behind. The victorious Reds make their way the short distance from Manchester's Central Station to the Town Hall, where crowds are waiting to cheer the new Cup winners. This was the first of 12 FA Cups won by the Reds and the whole city celebrated, with silverware for either United or City widely greeted with a sense of civic pride.

OLD MANCHESTER UNITED IN COLOUR

United captain Charlie Roberts leads out his team ahead of the Reds' first FA Cup final, against Bristol City on 24 April 1909. Behind him is full-back George Stacey, who goes on to play 270 matches (scoring nine goals) for the Reds between 1906-1915. The image also shows a policeman keeping back spectators in a section of the reported 71,401 crowd packed into the Crystal Palace stadium, London. During the game, Sandy Turnbull scores the only goal in the 22nd minute – the highlight of what is described as a dour spectacle in one newspaper match report. Those reports also pick out United's 'Welsh Wizard' Billy Meredith as the game's star performer, and make reference to an injury to left-back Vince Hayes who briefly has to leave the field with a broken rib – forcing United to play with 10 men – before returning to play in attack. However, Ernest Mangnall's Reds hold on to lift the Cup with a 1-0 win.

GLORY, GLORY

There was quite a wait for United's next FA Cup final... 39 years (and two world wars) to be precise! Pictured below is part of the pre-match presentation for the 1948 FA Cup final at Wembley, with Reds captain Johnny Carey introducing King George VI to his players – his royal highness shown shaking hands with centre-half Allenby Chilton. The two clubs are requested to wear their change kits for the final due to their home strips (red for United and tangerine for Blackpool) being deemed to clash. Keeping with traditions of the time, the United shirt includes the Manchester coat of arms for the final and the socks are changed to blue and white so as not to clash with Blackpool's black and white hooped 'stockings'. Played on 24 April 1948, and watched by 99,842, the final proves to be a classic: Matt Busby's side twice coming from behind to beat the Seasiders 4-2 thanks to three goals in the final 20 minutes.

OLD MANCHESTER UNITED IN COLOUR

GLORY, GLORY

King George VI hands over the FA Cup to skipper Johnny Carey at the end of the 1948 final, watched on by HRH Queen Elizabeth (on left) and Charlie Mitten (extreme right). The victory had been hard earned by United, falling behind to an Eddie Shimwell penalty, equalising through Jack Rowley, only to trail again to a Stan Mortensen strike 10 minutes before the break. And that's how it stayed until the final 20 minutes, when Matt Busby's formidable attacking line-up finally found their stride. Rowley darted between two defenders to head United level again from a quickly taken free-kick, Stan Pearson waltzed into the Blackpool box to fire in off the far post, with the 4-2 scoreline completed by a stunning long-range shot from John Anderson – all in the space of 12 minutes. It was the first trophy of Busby's glorious reign.

OLD MANCHESTER UNITED IN COLOUR

GLORY, GLORY

Captain Carey heads back to the Wembley pitch to continue the Cup-winning celebrations in April 1948, followed by his team-mates. Speaking to reporters afterwards, the Irishman said: "It was a hard fight right from the start. Blackpool's early goal served to make us more determined, and once we scored our second equaliser we all felt the supreme effort would bring the Cup to Manchester. Everyone gave it their best and it is a proud moment for me to say 'thank you' to all our supporters who have followed us through this wonderful season."

OLD MANCHESTER UNITED IN COLOUR

Carey and the Cup are held aloft by winger Charlie Mitten and goalkeeper Jack Crompton as United embark on a lap of honour around the Wembley pitch after the '48 final. Reds fans in the crowd gleefully chant "We won the Cup" as the players show their delight at winning English football's showpiece fixture. For Busby's team, this success was achieved after beating Aston Villa (6-4), Liverpool (3-0), Charlton Athletic (2-0), Preston North End (4-1), and Derby County (3-1) to reach the final – with none of the ties played at Old Trafford due the stadium not yet fit for use after bomb damage during the Second World War. Mitten, Carey and Crompton played in all six ties in the Cup triumph (Mitten scoring three goals), as the Reds landed the trophy for the second time.

GLORY, GLORY

Left: Skip forward to 1956 and Reds skipper Roger Byrne holds aloft the First Division trophy, won by the Busby Babes in glorious fashion. Behind Byrne are Johnny Berry, Duncan Edwards and David Pegg.

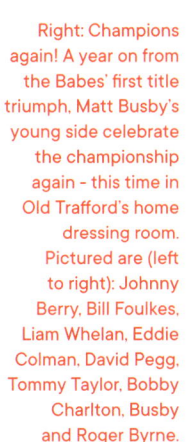

Right: Champions again! A year on from the Babes' first title triumph, Matt Busby's young side celebrate the championship again - this time in Old Trafford's home dressing room. Pictured are (left to right): Johnny Berry, Bill Foulkes, Liam Whelan, Eddie Colman, David Pegg, Tommy Taylor, Bobby Charlton, Busby and Roger Byrne.

OLD MANCHESTER UNITED IN COLOUR

GLORY, GLORY

Left: United and Leicester City emerge from the Wembley tunnel ahead of the 1963 FA Cup final, with Matt Busby's team donning fetching red tracksuit tops for the most eagerly anticipated fixture on the English football calendar.

Captains Noel Cantwell (United) and Colin Appleton (Leicester) shake hands as referee Ken Aston gets ready for the coin toss ahead of the FA Cup final, on 25 May 1963. On the way to the final – which is watched by a 99,604 crowd – the Reds had defeated Huddersfield Town, Aston Villa, Chelsea, Coventry and Southampton. Yet it was the Foxes who were favourites to lift the Cup having finished fourth in the First Division while the Reds ended the campaign way down in 19th place, just three points clear of relegation. However, Cup football is always unpredictable and Matt Busby's side finally fulfilled their potential – winning 3-1 thanks to goals from Denis Law and David Herd (2), Ken Keyworth grabbing a late consolation for Leicester. "I can't understand how that team finished where they did in the league," says Foxes skipper Appleton after the game. Busby expresses his delight that his star names have come good on the big occasion, for what is United's third FA Cup triumph.

That's what it means to win the Cup! United's players are delighted to have landed the FA Cup, the first trophy won by the club since before the Munich Air Disaster in 1958. Pictured are (left to right): Bobby Charlton, captain Noel Cantwell, Paddy Crerand, Albert Quixall and two-goal David Herd. In an era when few clubs wear a club crest on their shirt, the Manchester coat of arms is once again added to the Reds' Cup final jersey. With the game being shown live on television, Leicester are required (after losing a coin toss) to wear their white change strip for the game rather than their normal blue in order for viewers to more easily distinguish between the two sides in the black-and-white broadcast.

OLD MANCHESTER UNITED IN COLOUR

GLORY, GLORY

26 May 1963: Captain Cantwell shows off the Cup ahead of the train journey from London Euston back to Manchester, where a bus parade of the trophy awaits them. This is also the start of an exciting new journey for Busby's third great United side, although Cantwell will become more of a peripheral figure for the Reds as Tony Dunne emerges in his position. Two Football league titles and the European Cup will be won by the Reds over the next five years, with this Cup success later being viewed as a crucial stepping stone towards bringing the glory years back to Old Trafford.

OLD MANCHESTER UNITED IN COLOUR

GLORY, GLORY

13 May 1967: A packed Old Trafford cheers manager Matt Busby onto the pitch – with his players and officials from the Football League applauding – as United are crowned champions of England for a seventh time. Lining up to greet him are (l-r): David Herd (on crutches), John Aston (Jnr), Bobby Charlton, David Sadler, George Best, Nobby Stiles, Bill Foulkes, Paddy Crerand, Tony Dunne, Shay Brennan, Alex Stepney, Reds captain Denis Law, assistant secretary of the Football League Eric Howarth, past president of the Football League Sir Joseph Richards, current president of the Football League Len Shipman and United chairman Louis Edwards. Busby's side had won the title in the previous fixture, thrashing West Ham 6-1 at the Boleyn Ground, and on this afternoon against Stoke City would complete an unbeaten home league record of 17 wins and four draws across the season. The game was far from a thriller, ending goalless, but it was the sight of the Football League trophy back at Old Trafford that 60,071 had come for.

OLD MANCHESTER UNITED IN COLOUR

GLORY, GLORY

United captain Bobby Charlton, who is standing in for the injured club skipper Denis Law, exchanges pennants with Benfica captain Mario Coluna ahead of the European Cup final at Wembley, on 29 May 1968. With the Portuguese side designated the home team following a coin toss, they chose to wear white, but with television coverage still being black and white United are requested to wear dark shirts to make distinguishing between the teams easier for viewers. Busby's side choose to wear the third strip, a rich royal blue adorned with the Manchester coat of arms (as worn previously in FA Cup finals). United are huge favourites to overcome the ageing *As Aguias (the Eagles)*, but it proves to be a nerve-jangling first 90 minutes. Thankfully a joyous evening for majority of the 92,225 inside Wembley still awaits, thanks to a rampant Reds display in extra-time.

OLD MANCHESTER UNITED IN COLOUR

George Best celebrates just two minutes into extra-time of the 1968 European Cup final, setting the Reds on course to continental glory. Opponents Benfica had held United to a 1-1 draw over 90 minutes – Bobby Charlton's opener being levelled up by Jaime Graca with 11 minutes remaining – but any thoughts of momentum shifting to the Portuguese are soon dismissed. First, Best bursts clear, skips around goalkeeper Jose Enrique, then slides the ball into the empty net; two minutes later Brian Kidd heads in a rebound to make it 3-1; then Charlton adds his second in the 99th minute, stroking home a Kidd cross, to make it 4-1. The remainder of the game is played out in a celebratory atmosphere with cries of "We are the champions" from the huge Reds following at the Twin Towers. Emotional scenes greet the final whistle as Matt Busby's long held dream is finally realised.

● OLD MANCHESTER UNITED IN COLOUR

Matt Busby holds tightly to the trophy he'd coveted more than any other – and no wonder after spending over decade waiting to add the oversized cup to the Old Trafford honours board. Against Football League advice, he's taken his 1956 champions into the European Cup, being the first English team to enter the competition. Then came the tragic events of the Munich Air Disaster in February 1958, where eight of his continental cup hopefuls were killed returning from a European Cup quarter-final tie at Red Star Belgrade. Semi-final defeat in 1966 to unfancied Partizan Belgrade had been a bitter pill to swallow, but now, finally, Busby had landed the big one. Manchester United were kings of Europe at last, and here, on the night of the final, he enters the official party for the victory celebrations at the team's hotel in central London.

OLD MANCHESTER UNITED IN COLOUR

GLORY, GLORY

30 May 1968: The morning after the night before! Following the incredible events at Wembley the previous evening, Paddy Crerand, George Best and United manager Matt Busby show off the European Cup at Euston Station, ahead of boarding their train back to Manchester for a parade through the city. Flanked by police and security, the trio hold tight to the trophy so gloriously won against Benfica.

OLD MANCHESTER UNITED IN COLOUR

GLORY, GLORY

It would be eight years before United were next back at Wembley, but nine before enjoying success there. In the 1976 FA Cup final the Reds had slipped to a shock defeat to Southampton, with Tommy Docherty vowing to fans that his side would be back to win the trophy the following year. He was true to his word, and here is the proof: United skipper Martin Buchan lifting the Cup on 21 May 1977 following a 2-1 victory over fierce rivals Liverpool. Bob Paisley's Merseysiders were chasing the Treble, seeking to be the first club to achieve the feat. Instead, Doc's Reds were 2-1 victors thanks to goals from Stuart Pearson and Jimmy Greenhoff.

OLD MANCHESTER UNITED IN COLOUR

The celebrations after the 1977 Cup final victory were memorable, with this image showing (left to right); Stuart 'Pancho' Pearson, coach Tommy Cavanagh, manager Tommy Docherty, Lou Macari, Gordon Hill and assistant manager Frank Blunstone. This was the fourth time United had won the FA Cup, having also lost in three finals. The Reds would lose their next final in 1979 to Arsenal (2-3), but were then victorious in 1983 when Ron Atkinson's side beat Brighton & Hove Albion 4-0 in a Wembley replay.

GLORY, GLORY

OLD MANCHESTER UNITED IN COLOUR

GLORY, GLORY

While the 1985 FA Cup final between United and Everton was shown in colour on UK television, photographs in the next day's newspapers still appeared in monochrome. Like this image, which captures the decisive moment of the afternoon on 18 May 1985: Norman Whiteside shaping to curl the ball around Toffee's defender Pat van den Hauwe, beyond goalkeeper Neville Southall into the far corner of the net. The Northern Irishman's stunning winning goal, scored in the 110th minute for the 10-man Reds (Kevin Moran having been sent off in the 78th minute), is watched by almost 100,000 people inside Wembley and many millions more all around the world.

PICTURE INDEX

You've seen the full colourised images, but here is how they originally looked in black-and-white – plus details of the page they appear on and from where the photographs were sourced

Introduction

Page number: 10
Photo agency: Getty Images

Page number: 11
Photo agency: Getty Images

Page number: 12
Photo agency: Mirrorpix

Page number: 12
Photo agency: Getty Images

Page number: 13
Photo agency: Getty Images

Page number: 14
Photo agency: Alamy

Page number: 15
Photo agency: Mirrorpix

Match Action

Page number: 18
Photo agency: Getty Images

Page number: 19
Photo agency: Alamy

Page number: 20
Photo agency: Getty Images

Page number: 21
Photo agency: Alamy

Page number: 22
Photo agency: Getty Images

Page number: 22
Photo agency: Getty Images

Page number: 23
Photo agency: Getty Images

Page number: 24
Photo agency: Getty Images

Page number: 26
Photo agency: Getty Images

Page number: 28
Photo agency: Getty Images

Page number: 30
Photo agency: Mirrorpix

Page number: 31
Photo agency: Mirrorpix

Page number: 31
Photo agency: Alamy

Page number: 32
Photo agency: Colorsport

Page number: 34
Photo agency: Alamy

Page number: 34
Photo agency: Alamy

Page number: 35
Photo agency: Getty Images

Page number: 36
Photo agency: Getty Images

Page number: 37
Photo agency: Getty Images

Page number: 37
Photo agency: Alamy

Page number: 38
Photo agency: Getty Images

Page number: 38
Photo agency: Alamy

Page number: 40
Photo agency: Alamy

Old Trafford

Page number: **44**
Photo agency: Alamy

Page number: **45**
Photo agency: Alamy

Page number: **46**
Photo agency: Mirrorpix

Page number: **47**
Photo agency: Mirrorpix

Page number: **48**
Photo agency: Alamy

Page number: **50**
Photo agency: Mirrorpix

Page number: **52**
Photo agency: Getty Images

Page number: **53**
Photo agency: Getty Images

Page number: **54**
Photo agency: Mirrorpix

Page number: **54**
Photo agency: Alamy

Page number: **55**
Photo agency: Mirrorpix

The Fans

Page number: **58**
Photo agency: Mirrorpix

Page number: **59**
Photo agency: Alamy

Page number: **60**
Photo agency: Getty Images

Page number: **62**
Photo agency: Getty Images

Page number: 64
Photo agency: Getty Images

Page number: 66
Photo agency: Getty Images

Page number: 67
Photo agency: Getty Images

Page number: 68
Photo agency: Alamy

Page number: 70
Photo agency: Colorsport

Page number: 72
Photo agency: Alamy

Page number: 72
Photo agency: Mirrorpix

Page number: 73
Photo agency: Getty Images

Page number: 74
Photo agency: Alamy

Page number: 75
Photo agency: Getty Images

Page number: 75
Photo agency: Getty Images

Page number: 76
Photo agency: Mirrorpix

Page number: 77
Photo agency: Mirrorpix

Page number: 77
Photo agency: Alamy

Page number: 78
Photo agency: Getty Images

Page number: 80
Photo agency: Mirrorpix

Teams

Page number: **84**
Photo agency: Alamy

Page number: **85**
Photo agency: Alamy

Page number: **86**
Photo agency: Mirrorpix

Page number: **87**
Photo agency: Alamy

Page number: **88**
Photo agency: Getty Images

Page number: **88**
Photo agency: Getty Images

Page number: **89**
Photo agency: Getty Images

Page number: **90**
Photo agency: Getty Images

Page number: **92**
Photo agency: Getty Images

Page number: **94**
Photo agency: Getty Images

Page number: **96**
Photo agency: Alamy

Page number: **98**
Photo agency: Alamy

Page number: **100**
Photo agency: Alamy

Page number: **102**
Photo agency: Alamy

Page number: **102**
Photo agency: Colorsport

Page number: **103**
Photo agency: Colorsport

Page number: 103
Photo agency: Getty Images

Page number: 104
Photo agency: Getty Images

Page number: 106
Photo agency: Getty Images

Page number: 106
Photo agency: Colorsport

Page number: 107
Photo agency: Getty Images

Page number: 108
Photo agency: Getty Images

Page number: 110
Photo agency: Alamy

Page number: 110
Photo agency: Getty Images

Page number: 111
Photo agency: Alamy

Page number: 112
Photo agency: Mirrorpix

Page number: 114
Photo agency: Getty Images

The Players

Page number: 118
Photo agency: Getty Images

Page number: 119
Photo agency: Mirrorpix

Page number: 120
Photo agency: Getty Images

Page number: 121
Photo agency: Mirrorpix

→ The Players (continued)

Page number: **122**
Photo agency: Getty Images

Page number: **122**
Photo agency: Getty Images

Page number: **122**
Photo agency: Getty Images

Page number: **123**
Photo agency: Getty Images

Page number: **124**
Photo agency: Getty Images

Page number: **125**
Photo agency: Getty Images

Page number: **125**
Photo agency: Alamy

Page number: **126**
Photo agency: Alamy

Page number: **126**
Photo agency: Alamy

Page number: **127**
Photo agency: Alamy

Page number: **128**
Photo agency: Alamy

Page number: **129**
Photo agency: Mirrorpix

Page number: **130**
Photo agency: Colorsport

Page number: **132**
Photo agency: Colorsport

Page number: **133**
Photo agency: Getty Images

Page number: **134**
Photo agency: Mirrorpix

Page number: **135**
Photo agency: Mirrorpix

Page number: **136**
Photo agency: Mirrorpix

Page number: **137**
Photo agency: Getty Images

Page number: **138**
Photo agency: Mirrorpix

Page number: 139
Photo agency: Getty Images

Page number: 139
Photo agency: Getty Images

Page number: 140
Photo agency: Alamy

Page number: 142
Photo agency: Getty Images

Page number: 144
Photo agency: Alamy

Page number: 145
Photo agency: Alamy

Page number: 146
Photo agency: Colorsport

Page number: 146
Photo agency: Getty Images

Page number: 147
Photo agency: Getty Images

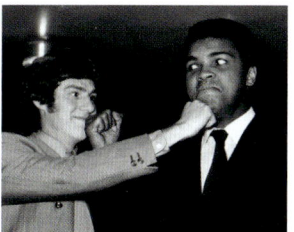

Page number: 147
Photo agency: Alamy

Page number: 148
Photo agency: Getty Images

Page number: 149
Photo agency: Getty Images

Page number: 150
Photo agency: Getty Images

Page number: 152
Photo agency: Getty Images

Page number: 153
Photo agency: Alamy

Page number: 153
Photo agency: Colorsport

Page number: 154
Photo agency: Getty Images

Page number: 155
Photo agency: Getty Images

Page number: 156
Photo agency: Getty Images

Page number: 158
Photo agency: Getty Images

→ # The Players (continued)

Page number: 160
Photo agency: Getty Images

Page number: 161
Photo agency: Getty Images

Page number: 162
Photo agency: Getty Images

Page number: 164
Photo agency: Getty Images

Page number: 165
Photo agency: Getty Images

Page number: 166
Photo agency: Alamy

Page number: 167
Photo agency: Getty Images

Page number: 168
Photo agency: Getty Images

Page number: 168
Photo agency: Getty Images

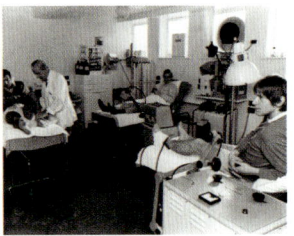
Page number: 169
Photo agency: Getty Images

Page number: 170
Photo agency: Mirrorpix

Page number: 171
Photo agency: Getty Images

Page number: 172
Photo agency: Alamy

Busby's Babes

Page number: 176
Photo agency: Getty Images

Page number: 178
Photo agency: Getty Images

Page number: 179
Photo agency: Getty Images

Page number: 180
Photo agency: Getty Images

Page number: 182
Photo agency: Colorsport

Page number: 183
Photo agency: Getty Images

Page number: 183
Photo agency: Getty Images

Page number: 184
Photo agency: Alamy

Page number: 186
Photo agency: Colorsport

Page number: 188
Photo agency: Alamy

Page number: 189
Photo agency: Mirrorpix

Page number: 190
Photo agency: Getty Images

Page number: 192
Photo agency: Mirrorpix

Page number: 194
Photo agency: Alamy

Page number: 195
Photo agency: Alamy

Page number: 196
Photo agency: Alamy

Page number: 198
Photo agency: Getty Images

Managers

Page number: 202
Photo agency: Mirrorpix

Page number: 203
Photo agency: Getty Images

Page number: 204
Photo agency: Mirrorpix

Page number: 206
Photo agency: Mirrorpix

Page number: 208
Photo agency: Getty Images

Page number: 210
Photo agency: Getty Images

Page number: 211
Photo agency: Mirrorpix

Page number: 212
Photo agency: Colorsport

Page number: 213
Photo agency: Alamy

Page number: 214
Photo agency: Getty Images

Page number: 216
Photo agency: Mirrorpix

Page number: 218
Photo agency: Mirrorpix

Page number: 220
Photo agency: Getty Images

Page number: 221
Photo agency: Alamy

Page number: 222
Photo agency: Getty Images

Page number: 224
Photo agency: Alamy

Page number: 226
Photo agency: Getty Images

Page number: 228
Photo agency: Getty Images

Page number: 230
Photo agency: Alamy

Page number: 232
Photo agency: Mirrorpix

Page number: 234
Photo agency: Mirrorpix

Page number: 236
Photo agency: Mirrorpix

Glory, Glory

Page number: 240
Photo agency: Getty Images

Page number: 242
Photo agency: Mirrorpix

Page number: 243
Photo agency: Alamy

Page number: 244
Photo agency: Getty Images

Page number: 246
Photo agency: Getty Images

Page number: 247
Photo agency: Getty Images

Page number: 248
Photo agency: Alamy

Page number: 250
Photo agency: Getty Images

→ Glory (continued)

Page number: **252**
Photo agency: Getty Images

Page number: **253**
Photo agency: Getty Images

Page number: **253**
Photo agency: Getty Images

Page number: **254**
Photo agency: Getty Images

Page number: **255**
Photo agency: Colorsport

Page number: **256**
Photo agency: Mirrorpix

Page number: **258**
Photo agency: Getty Images

Page number: **260**
Photo agency: Mirrorpix

Page number: **262**
Photo agency: Getty Images

Page number: **264**
Photo agency: Getty Images

Page number: **266**
Photo agency: Getty Images

Page number: **268**
Photo agency: Alamy

Page number: **270**
Photo agency: Alamy

Page number: **272**
Photo agency: Alamy

Page number: **274**
Photo agency: Getty Images